DISCOVERING THE DEPTHS

William Clemmons is Professor of Christian Education at Southeastern Baptist Theological Seminary in North Carolina, where he also teaches courses in spirituality. Prior to joining the faculty in 1979 he served in various ministries as a pastor, missionary and director of the Vineyard Conference Centre in Louisville, Kentucky. He is a popular retreat leader in the United States, particularly in the areas of prayer and spiritual growth.

Discovering the Depths

William Clemmons

TRiANGLE

Triangle
SPCK
Holy Trinity Church
Marylebone Road
London NW1 4DU

First published in the USA by Broadman Press
First published in Great Britain by Triangle Books 1989

British Library Cataloguing in Publication Data
Clemmons, William, *1932*–
    Discovering the depths.
    1. Christian life. Meditation. Prayer.
    Meditation and prayer
    I. Title
    248.3

    ISBN 0–281–04414–7

Photoset by Inforum Typesetting, Portsmouth
Printed in Great Britain by
Hazell, Watson & Viney Ltd
Aylesbury Bucks

Contents

Introduction

Discovering the Depths is intended for persons who are seeking serious guidance in their personal spiritual growth. There is a real hunger in society among persons who are looking for help with their inner lives. This area has not been adequately dealt with in academic or Christian education. Today many voices are seeking to correct that situation.

This book in no way seeks to be exhaustive or conclusive in spiritual guidance. All I have attempted to do is to set down some of the areas of a formative process of spiritual growth which have been valuable to Christians over the centuries.

Interest in my own spiritual growth prompted my writing this book in the first place. My first formal explorations in spirituality were guided by Father Augustine Wulff, OCSO (1899–1985), a Trappist monk of Gethesemani Monastery in Kentucky. Later, I had the chance to explore this area in a more systematic fashion at the Institute of Formative Spirituality, Duquesne University, in Pittsburgh, Pennsylvania, one of the many places seeking to develop a comprehensive theory of Christian spirituality.[1] And, since 1979 I have offered courses in spirituality at Southeastern Baptist Theological Seminary.

Spiritual formation is not a reduction of human life to the spiritual, but an integration of *all dimensions* of human personality around the most fundamental dimension, that of being made in the image and likeness of God (*imago dei*). This fundamental dimension of human personality is most characteristically experienced as the potential of being godwardly drawn. However, one experiences life as 'less than' when life is not integrated around the transcendent dimension of human personality. Because life is experienced as a quest for the 'more than', and as illusive when not grounded in this foundational aspect of self, one seeks to go beyond, to be whole, to know the 'true self'. These are all expressions of this drawing of persons to that deepest centre within, which is fulfilled only as it acknowledges and yields all of life to this deepest integration around the foundational form of life.

Therefore, spiritual formation is not seeking to make one *conform* to a predetermined mould in which all followers of Christ must be pressed into some divine 'cookie cutter' process. It is more a journey into deeper and deeper dimensions of what it means individually and collectively to be God's people in a world like ours. Each brings his or her own preformation dispositions to the task. And each one uniquely expresses the form that God wishes that one to work with in the diversity that makes up the pluralism of gifts in the church.

This work of spiritual formation is a costly work of daily recognizing illusions about ourselves and responding to the call of God to discipleship in a world like ours. It is a call to a co-creative relationship with God in being fully alive in Christ. It is a call to live life at the deepest level of our potentiality in Christ. And it is a call to join God in a work of ministry and witness at the deepest level of our co-creativity with Him.

Spiritual formation is a living of the Christian life as an adventure of faith, never quite sure of tomorrow, but knowing Him who will direct us in that step into tomorrow. It is a journey of both giving and receiving form for our lives. One is called to receive formative life directives from transcendent sources, from inward dialogue with all dimensions of life, from life lived in relationships, from daily living, from the current world setting, from our faith traditions, and especially from Scripture. One then also gives form to each of these areas of life.

It is a journey that often understands the work of God that occurred yesterday as distance and formative reflection begins to make its own patchwork quilt out of the daily pilgrimage. It is a journey lived into the depths of today with the fullest consciousness of our being attuned, aware, and responsive to what God is doing now.

Spiritual formation is thus a call into an inward journey—a journey where the inner work of God is done in such a depth that the results of this deep encounter are experienced in a changed self, a commitment to deal with irrelevant structures of the church and society, and to a ministry and witness to the brokenness of society. The roots of a genuine renewal of the life of any person or congregation are more than externals (re-formation) for it is based on that which only God can do (trans-formation) with us. Both are necessary, but God's work is foundational.

This book is directed, therefore, toward helping you explore your 'unique-self-in-Christ' through a process of being opened up to new levels of your journey in Christ. It will seek to help you examine at a deeper level what it means to be the people of God today. By discoverying the depths of God and the depths of yourself, you may find the point where these two converge into a new and more dynamic self-in-Christ.

My hope for you as you read each chapter and do the meditation assignment which accompanies it is that this can be for you a twelve-week spiritual-growth experience. I hope that it will help you develop with God a more adequate response to who you are in Christ and how this is lived out in your relationships with others, in daily living, and in the context of the current world setting. My larger hope is that as you experience the transformation work of God it will become the basis of a radical renewal of God's people that is equal to the needs of the society in which we live. This can be a twelve-week journey into new and mysterious depths of Christian growth and maturity by which God can release you in a powerful ministry and witness to the brokenness of the world.

Each chapter examines an element of an ever-deepening life in Christ. It first describes that dimension and is followed by a meditative experience that is to be done for thirty minutes each day for that week. Each element and meditative assignment forms part of what could be for you the basis of a continuing personal, daily meditative life at the end of the twelve weeks.

This book is not intended to be a book of 'devotional ideas' which seek only to inspire and be a morning pep pill which by afternoon has worn off. Serious spiritual growth is costly and gradual. It is the work of a lifetime. It is the work of just the right amount of personal effort, awaiting God's response of grace. There are many times when we just wait until God is ready for us to make the next step.

Therefore, this book is intended for slow, careful meditative reflection. It is not to be read or digested in two or three sittings. It is designed to lead you slowly along a journey into increasingly deeper dimensions of yourself, your relationship with God and others. Therefore, I would suggest that you *not* plan to read more than a chapter a week, pausing each day to work with that part of the meditative assignment for the day.

Maybe you will find it helpful to reread the chapter several times during the week, pausing to reflect on a section that has caught your attention. Reflect on it—what is its deeper meaning for you? How do you respond to it—with a *resonance*—or a resistance? If a sentence or a paragraph strikes you in a particular way, stop reading, your reflection has begun. You do not have to get through the book in a day, a week, a month, or even a year.

Allow your mind and the deeper work of the Holy Spirit to guide you further and deeper into the meanings for you that lie below the surface. Then and only then will you be able to say that your meditations have begun. As long as you ask a book to do your thinking for you, you have escaped the responsibility for that intimate dialogue between you and God. But, once a passage grabs you, the dialogue has begun.

It is often helpful to keep a written record of what happens in your daily meditations. Therefore, at the end of each chapter is a section called 'Meditation Exercises'. Use a separate notebook to work in. This will become the written record of what occurs in your spiritual journey.[2] It is a valuable tool for getting below the surface of your life and what you've been experiencing. You should record daily the thoughts you've had and the *movement of God* in your life as you've been able to discern it for that day. Daily assignments at the end of each chapter will help you with your writing. Follow them, adding anything else you experience in your journey with God each day. It is for your eyes alone, so be as honest as you can. This can be the basis of sharing later with a spiritual director.[3]

A daily 'quiet time' is necessary if you are to work seriously with your personal spiritual growth. More will be said about this in Chapter 5. For now, all you need do is set aside some time each day to work on the meditative assignments at the end of each chapter. Find a place where you will not be disturbed for the time you are working with the assignment and where you can be still and reflective for the time you've allotted to work with it.

I wrote this book a decade ago. I have been surprised at its usefulness to so many people in many different walks of life around the world. I am pleased that this revised edition is appearing at the requests and encouragements of those who have affirmed its usefulness. A special word of thanks goes to

Mrs Carolyn Bailey who typed the revised manuscript.

May this prayer be your guide as you work with the material in this book. It is my hope for you:

> O Lord,
> there are depths within me
> I would like to touch;
> and there are depths of your Presence
> I would like to experience.
> Surrender within me, O Lord,
> these new depths
> as I give myself up in loving obedience
> to your holy creativity. AMEN

Wake Forest, NC
Fall 1986

1

The Inner Work of God

People today seek deeper meanings about themselves and the world in order to re-invent and re-imagine a new kind of world. This need affects Christians and the church as much as any other group today. Seeking assurances amid turbulent change has led too many to affirm old solutions of the eighteenth and nineteenth centuries, regardless of whether those solutions are any more adequate than trying to go from Lascassas to Nashville on Interstate 24 in my grandfather's horse and buggy.

This revisioning process is being assisted today through renewed understandings of a Christian life-style and the concept of authentic selfhood. The word *life-style* came into usage in this century to describe the way a life is oriented, based on expressed or unexpressed values and meanings which manifest themselves in such things as the clothes we wear, the food we eat, the way we comb our hair, the friends we associate with, the very furniture we have in our houses. All of these things say something about our life-style.

Alfred Adler, the psychologist who coined the word *life-style*, saw it as an essential clue in helping persons understand why life was directed in certain ways. If one adopted a life-style in which all of one's energies were spent in buying just the right clothes, arranging the house with just the right pieces, it might be said that a person had a certain type of life-style. If on the other hand one wore clothes that were in style ten years ago, drove a ten-year-old car, and bought only furniture that could be purchased at auctions, garage sales, and used furniture stores, it might be said one had another kind of life-style.

There is a 'language' about the way we live. It can be seen in our clothes, the way we speak and don't speak to persons, in our eyes, mouth, the way of walking, everything about us. Today there is a genuine search for life-style which speaks of a new kind of people of God.

Jesus spent much time working with the disciples to help them distinguish between relevant and irrelevant life-styles. He helped them adopt a way of living which spoke of inner realities. He admonished them to beware of the 'leaven of the Pharisees' (Matt. 16.6, KJV). He guided them in discussions of what was of value and what was not. He even involved them in conflict with the then-existing customs of hand-washing and sabbath observances.

Jesus made it plain that what was being asked for was an outward manifestation of living which was in harmony with deep inner life directives—a Christian life-style. The real work of a Christian life-style begins inwardly. Some would have us believe that if we would only rearrange the outward we would have won the battle. Yet when we return to the quiet centre of our being, we find that the battle continues to rage within, though we have performed the right outward acts. Consequently we have become wary of schemes which promise happiness and peace in five easy steps or victory through four laws or fullness in eleven basic convictions or even obedience to some chain of command. As Elizabeth O'Connor wrote: 'What is essential for authentic life lies within and our awakening to this is our awakening to life in Jesus Christ. "When the Spirit of truth comes, he will guide you into all the truth." '[1]

The costly work of a Christian life-style, then, involves the quest for a more *authentic selfhood*, found in the inner work of God. It is a work of discovering the inner reality of who we are in Christ, of being guided by and responding to the nudgings of the Holy Spirit. It may be that our first step is in response to the outward tensions we are experiencing in our current life situation. The first step brings us to an inner conviction and redirection of life in new and unknown areas. Or, our seeking a new direction may begin after a time of reflective meditation on the Scriptures. The Word of God may ignite a willingness to follow God's path for us. Or, it may start with the willingness to let go of an older reality about ourselves which allows us to embrace a new and emerging understanding, which is, then, lived out in a new way.

Though the emergence of a Christian life-style is from within, it must be expressed outwardly. At this point there is no disagreement. We must be careful, however, in starting with the outer rearrangements only, especially when they correspond to no inner reality. Then Christian life-style becomes nothing more than a rearrangement of externals which ends up in producing actions out of a sense of ought-ness, must, have-to, or should. And that, said Jesus, is loading persons with 'intolerable burdens' (Luke 11.46) and making only disciples of duty, not freedom or abundant living.

Thus, the work of a Christian life-style lies both within us and without. But the foundational work is from within, the inner work of God which shapes and moulds us for the new. John Sanford said:

> The whole self is in each of us as a potentiality and seeks to be realized in the life process. Our dreams express the urge to the realization of the whole man within us, and give us the insight into this inner world of which we are ordinarily unaware. In order for the realization of the whole personality to take place, however, the ego must

3

come into a creative relationship with the inner life, and be constantly expanding in order to give greater and greater expression to the whole scope of the personality.[2]

Thomas Merton also spoke of the inner work of God, but in terms of the true self and the false self.

We have the choice of two identities: the external mask which seems to be real and which lives by a shadowy autonomy for the brief moment of earthly existence, and the hidden inner person who seems to us to be nothing, but who can give himself externally to the truth in whom he subsists.[3]

The false self wears the mask. It is the one I present to you out of fear that you may not like the real me. Soon I spend all of my time cultivating the mask while the real me dries up and withers away. Before long, even I come to believe that the mask is the real me, and I forget the real self hidden away in the deep, dark recess of my inner chambers.

Then one day someone gives me the chance to lower the mask just a little and I discover it for what it really is—play-acting; something that, all along, was not me. Afraid to be me, I had looked around for the person who was liked and admired by everyone, and I had tried to become that person so others would like me also. In so doing, my unique self was never allowed to live, to be known and loved by 'them'. All they ever saw was the carbon copy of the other one they loved, and they never had a chance to love the real me.

The true self is the self that I am meant to be. It is the self I am able to work with God in creating, so that my own life, my own identity, my own destiny becomes possible. Because I am free and a child of God, I am invited, as are you, by Him to participate in the creation of my own life through the choices He gives me. This is a more costly approach for, said

Merton, it involves risk, sacrifice, anguish, and many tears as He reveals Himself

> in the mystery of each new situation. We do not know clearly beforehand what the results of this work will be. The secret of my full identity is hidden in Him. He alone can make me who I am, or rather who I will be when at last I fully begin to be. But unless I desire this identity and work to find it with Him and in Him, the work will never be done.[4]

Thus, the true self emerges as God and we actively work together in the creative freedom He has given us. A person who says erroneously, 'I've got to get out of the way in order for God to act', though he is struggling to explain a Christian insight, comes very close to saying that persons, created in the image of God, are of no worth. Such a declaration is a blasphemy since it maligns God's creation. What God wants is to co-operate, co-create with us in the creation of the truth of our lives. He is *not* saying to us that our self is of no worth. If that were so, God could have created robots so He could manipulate and override their personalities and wills.

What God did create were persons in His image. As the psalmist said, 'You have made him little less than a god, you have crowned him with glory and splendour, made him lord over the work of your hands, set all things under his feet' (Ps. 8.5–6, JB). That image has been falsified by the mask of the false self and our unwillingness to be the true selves that God created us to become. So, we say with Merton, 'To say I was born in sin is to say I came into the world with a false self. I was born in a mask. I came into existence under a sign of contradiction, being someone that I was never intended to be and therefore a denial of what I am supposed to be.'[5] To be in Christ, then, is to be the self that God knows and to cease to be the self that God knows nothing about. We are new creatures and have been called to the fullness of abundant life.

Those who would evade the responsibility of working with God in the creation of their own identities in Christ often say that they have to get out of the way so that God can be on the throne. Paul said, 'I have been put to death with Christ on his cross, so that it is no longer I who live, but it is Christ who lives in me. This life I live now, I live by faith in the Son of God, who loved me and gave his life for me' (Gal. 2.19–20, GNB). Many have taken this Pauline passage out of context and have cast it into a new gnosticism which denies the true worth of persons. I am sure that many do not realize what they are saying when they say, 'I want to get out of the way, so God can do something here tonight'. It often sounds like humility, disclaiming any part in what is happening. But it is a false humility and ends up disclaiming the role of working with God in that work to which He has called us.

I think J.B. Phillips more correctly translated Paul's intent: '[As far as the Law is concerned I may consider that] I died on the cross with Christ. And my present life is not that of the old "I", but the living Christ within me. The bodily life I now live, I live believing in the Son of God who loved me and sacrificed himself for me' (Gal. 2.19–20, Phillips). What Paul said was that the legalistic way of living had ended with Christ on the cross. The false self ended, and the true self takes a new shape in Christ.

Another passage often misused in this regard is the statement of John the Immerser, 'He must increase, but I must decrease' (John 3.30, RSV). These words have been used to downgrade the self. John knew who he was (though there is an indication that, as he lay in a Roman prison, he later wondered about the popular Jewish expectation that the Messiah would become the military liberator of Israel from foreign rule), for he said to the Jews, 'I am not the Messiah; I have been sent as his forerunner' (John 3.28, NEB). John's identity was never mixed up at that point. He was in touch with his true self. He was the forerunner. Jesus was the Messiah.

Therefore, to use John's words, one must be sure of her true self before she can say where that places her in relationship to Christ. In God's economy, John's ministry as forerunner had ended. He had been sent to prepare the way (Luke 3.4ff.). When Jesus was ready to commence His ministry and build on John's preparation, John then was ready to declare his ministry at an end. Only when we have come to the point in our lives where we are ready to consign our work to another, at the end of a particular work or at death, can we relinquish our ministry responsibility. Until then, we must continue our work as co-labourers with Christ.

The third passage about the self that is often misused is found in the words of Jesus regarding the conditions of discipleship. He said:

> If anyone wishes to be a follower of mine, he must leave self behind; he must take up his cross and come with me. Whoever cares for his own safety is lost; but if a man will let himself be lost for my sake, he will find his true self. What will a man gain by winning the whole world, at the cost of his true self? Or what can he give that will buy that self back? (Matt. 16.24–26, NEB).

All three Gospel writers reported that statement in the context of Jesus' announcement to the twelve that He would have to suffer and die. Peter's misunderstanding of Jesus' mission, 'We will not let this happen to you' (Matt. 16.22), and Jesus' bold denunciation of Peter for hindering the will of God, led to the statement about the costliness of discipleship. So, it would seem that those who quote this verse to deny their self-worth have chosen a verse out of context.

Jesus' whole concern about the role of the self was in relationship to the costliness of the gospel. Frank Stagg said of this passage.

> By forfeiting life, Jesus did not refer to physical death, for that comes to all. He referred to one's missing his true destiny, failing to become the self he was designed to be. For the *return* of his life, or in exchange for his lost selfhood, one would gladly give the world, could that be done. To state it more simply, as one pursues his goals in life, he may miss the true life which can be known alone in proper relationship with God.[6]

Thus, our basic sin may not be in self-love, in self-trust, or in self-esteem. Our sin is found in loving the false self, in trusting the false self, and in thinking highly of the self that does not know its existence in God. We are in love with the self that God did not create. We become ourselves when we lose the false selves to Christ (literally *die* to the false selves) and rise to the true selves in Christ. We cannot become our true selves except in Christ, the self that God the Creator intended us to be.

Many psychologists have described the need for persons to have a healthy self-concept. Those who work in the area of ego psychology have discovered that a person who thinks little of himself is a person less able to function well in what he does. There is a difference between ego-strength and egoism. The first has to do with a strong inner sense of identity while the latter has to do with a viewpoint that sees all of the world as centred around *me*.

The person who has taken the road of dealing with the inner identity of who he is has to deal at many points with the true and false self. He has to deal with the self and the non-self, the description of the distinguishing characteristics of one's self, one's values, and one's basic central perceptions. In other words, he has to deal with many of the features that make up the central core of his being.

The biblical understanding about the need for a strong concept of the true self is often described in the love of self (quoted from Lev. 19.18) by the lawyer who sought to tempt Jesus about which was the greatest commandment. Part of that answer was, 'You shall love your neighbour as yourself' (Mark 12.31, RSV). Self-love, or the appreciation of the worth of one's own self, is the beginning of love for neighbour. When one is able to diminish one's own self-hate and self-depreciation, one is more likely to stop hating and ridiculing one's neighbour. Also, the love for self and neighbour will enable one to love God better. As John said: 'If someone says he loves God, but hates his brother, he is a liar. For he cannot love God, whom he has not seen, if he does not love his brother, whom he has seen' (1 John 4.20, GNB).

Thus the real self, the self that is our journey into becoming, the real meaning of being 'in Christ,' is more than psychological self-realization. However, self-actualization remains a part truth for a follower of Christ. It may help in describing the person behind the mask, but it has not dealt sufficiently with the foundational question that the person in Christ must deal with, namely, what does it mean to stop being a self-sufficient, go-it-alone self and become a person who is willing to take up his cross daily and follow Christ? For the Christian, that is a work that he and God must do together.

To grow into our true selves is a labour requiring time. A lifetime is too short to complete it. It begins in the choices, the opportunities, God gives us. And if we can be free enough to let go of the falsity within us—the masks we play with—then in the liberty of each moment of each day, God and we can co-create our new identity. Thomas Merton wrote:

The seeds that are planted in my liberty at every moment, by God's will, are the seeds of my own identity, my own reality, my own happiness, my own sanctity. To refuse them is to refuse everything; it is the refusal of my own existence and being; of my identity, my very self. Not to accept and love and do God's will is to refuse the fullness of my existence. If I never become what I am meant to be but always remain what I am not, I shall spend eternity contradicting myself by being at once something and nothing, a life that wants to live and is dead, a death that wants to be dead and cannot quite achieve its own death because it still has to exist.[7]

God calls us to this lifetime vocation, which Paul called 'working out your own salvation with fear and trembling' (Phil. 2.12). It is a labour with Christ in working with the inner landscape of our own lives. Out of that material emerges truly Christian life-styles that are not built on outward conformity to certain rules of do's and don't's. Life-styles are fashioned on an inner working with the gospel, so that there is an outward conformity to an inner reality, the reality of our true selves in Christ.

The inner work of God in the unfolding of the true self involves three movements. The first is the call to wholeness. The biblical words, both Hebrew and Greek, which have been translated into English as 'salvation' have their roots in the words *health*, or *wholeness*. Since too often the word *salvation* is given only the meaning of deliverance or 'saved from', we miss the richness of God's call to salvation as a *call to wholeness*. His call to every person is to be truly whole, to be all that He intends one to be.

Wholeness means to allow the true self within us to begin to emerge, to be known, and to have its own existence in Christ affirmed. It means being more relaxed, released, creative, risking, resourceful, slowed down, receptive, and focused. It means being less a person who is straining, always playing it safe, busy with things, living out of the tyranny of oughts, shoulds and have-to's, going it alone, and closed.

Wholeness means dealing with that within us which keeps us from being free to follow Christ's faintest whisper. Meister Eckhart wrote: 'There are plenty to follow our Lord halfway, but not the other half. They will give up possessions, friends, and honours, but it touches them too closely to disown themselves.'[8] The true self within us wants to let go, but what of the false self within us that will not let go of us? Why are we not free? What keeps us in prison?

It's too easy just to say that sin keeps us from being free. When we've confessed all of our known sins, we still don't move. The roots of our non-freedom are much deeper than external acts of misbehaviour. The eradication of those roots is much more costly than most of us have imagined. They go to the very foundation of who we think ourselves to be, or try to be.

For most of us, our lack of freedom to follow God's good pleasure is not in unconfessed sins or in little acts of disobedience. They are but the signs of the battle within. The self that Christ came to set free and allow to become in us wrestles with that self within us which is unfaithful to God's greatest potential within us, our true self. We are a living contradiction within. Paul's description of this inward struggle helps us understand our own inward violence:

What I do is not what I want to do, but what I detest. . . . for though the will to do good is there, the deed is not. The good which I want to do, I fail to do; but what I do is the wrong which is against my will . . . clearly it is no longer I who am the agent, but sin that has its lodging in me. I discover the principle, then: that when I want to do right, only the wrong is within my reach. In my inmost self I delight in the law of God, but I perceive that there is in my

11

bodily members a different law, fighting against the law that my reason approves and making me a prisoner under the law that is in my members, the law of sin (Rom. 7.15, 18–23, NEB).

Paul's conclusion was that, because this battle is there, we are not to give up, resigning ourselves as hopelessly doomed. We know that in Jesus Christ 'the life-giving law of the Spirit has set you free from that law of sin and death' (Rom. 8.2, NEB).

We should not see the true self as the soul and the false self as the body. This would be the docetic misunderstanding that the body is not real while the soul is real. The conclusion from that would be that God loves only the soul and despises the body. The soul and the body are one close-knit unity and cannot be divided up. When Paul talked about things of the spirit and things of the body, he described those things which are Spirit-dominated and those things which are body-dominated. Here he used the body-dominated phrase to speak of what I am calling the false self, the self which goes it alone without God, the self that says, 'I can do it all by myself!'

Merton said, 'My false and private self is the one who wants to exist outside the reach of God's will and God's love—outside of reality and outside of life. And such a self cannot help but be an illusion.'[9] The emergence of the true self is not by our efforts alone: It is also the gift of God who encourages, calls us, and allows us to be with grace-gifts.

To remain in slavery is to remain chained to our false selves, afraid to experience the freedom that Christ offers us in the wholeness of new creation in Christ. It means exploring the chains in the inner chambers of our hearts. That which chains us is not found in the external acts as much as within ourselves. We are not free to be our true selves because we do not allow God's wholeness to do its work deep down within.

The person who acknowledges Jesus as Lord makes a commitment to living life fully. The chains that lie rusting in the dungeons of our hearts will slowly be unlocked one at a time over a lifetime as a commitment to wholeness and deliverance at a deeper level is worked out with fear and trembling. Certain habits which we seem unable to break may find their chains connected to the deeper root of 'being accepted in the crowd'. Greed may find its rusting iron hasps wound tightly to a childhood full of deprivations.

Little or no real journey into wholeness and healing is done without the inner work of God. He helps us in deep meditative reflection, under the guidance of the Holy Spirit, to reflect on the mystery of our own lives. Those who continue to live without the release of the true self risk making externals the badges of a Christian life-style which has no correspondence to inner truths. Living the Christian life becomes a burden—a matter of duty more than love. That life of do's and don't's has not become authentic *within*. It only conforms *without*.

Wholeness is a plunging into our inner sanctuary where the true, inner self can be gradually released in Christ; where we can come to terms with the true self in Christ; where the power of the false self can be diminished; where the shadowy dimension of our lives can be healed by the power of the Holy Spirit; where the dross can be purged and pure gold can become the basis of living life as gift; where our gifts for ministry and witness can be released in a community that loves and cares for us; and where we can be sufficiently detached and reflective of the world around us so that we are aware of where and how we have been shaped by it.

Then, as we are engaged in the redemptive-creative work of Christ in our lives, which comes from within (the renewing from within of which Paul spoke in Romans 12.2), we will also enter into a loving dialogue with the world, giving shape to it through God's redemptive hope, and allowing it to become God's home. This is the call to wholeness.

The second movement of the inner work of God focuses on a call to discover God's presence at increasingly deeper levels of our relationship with Him. The inner work of God is dynamic, not one-dimensional. As we uncover new depths of our true selves, we are also uncovering a deepening relationship with the Living God. Many drawn to those psychologies that promised to deal with the 'self' in a movement from health into more health have too often stopped short of a full self-discovery and self-actualization because they have not dealt seriously enough with the self-that-is-in-Christ. Therefore, they have neglected the transcendent dimension of self-realization.

Many have sought this transcendent dimension of self through Oriental religions, mysticism, drug-induced experiences, transcendental meditation, yoga, or attraction to the occult. The hunger for the intuitive, affective, or experiential dimension of the Transcendent in religious experience is evident as people continue to search in extraordinary ways for this element which has been missing in much of Western Christianity.

The need to know at deep experiential levels the realities of the Christian faith, unapproachable through ordinary means of reasoning, is acute among serious Christians today. What they seek is an intuitive, trans-conscious, contemplative approach to life. The transcendent dimension of human personality, which pushes many to seek God at deeper levels of their lives, is a search for a religion of the heart, as well as of the mind. It is a search for an experiencing of God at the deepest levels of their being, a search which does not manifest itself in super-emotionalism or super-rationalism. It is a longing for an experience of the faintest whisper of God found in silence and the deepest recesses of personal, inner solitude.

14

Prayer too often means nothing more than, 'Lord give me this. Lord give me that.' For many, prayer has become nothing more than another religious activity, a duty to be fulfilled. Instead prayer needs to be seen as the discovery of God at deeper and deeper levels of relationship, a conversation between two friends. Orthodox Christianity speaks of 'praying with your mind in your heart'. It is the prayer of the heart that allows a person to discover at deeper recesses of one's being this prayer relationship with God.

Eastern Christianity describes three levels of prayer. First, there is the level of vocal prayer, those set prayers which we use at meal time, at meetings and in church services, or when we pray using any prayer formula. These may be the words that we use to express the thanksgivings or petitions of the moment on behalf of ourselves and others. Since vocal prayer was the first mode of praying that we were taught as children—'Now I lay me down to sleep' or 'God is great, God is good, let us thank Him for our food'—many find it very difficult to know any other type of prayer life. Because we simply lack skills and training in the deeper, experiential dimensions of prayer, we have never progressed beyond vocal prayers.

The second level of prayer is called mental prayer, for it involves the mind and conscious activity of reflection. In it we involve both reason and intellect. This is the type of praying which is found when we meditate. For instance, as we pray meditatively, our rational and thinking processes may be focused on the life of Christ and how it speaks to our lives at deeper and deeper levels.

The last level of prayer, called prayer of the heart, experiences God at the deepest level of our being. It is prayer where the mind is not just a rational instrument, but becomes integrated in the person so deeply that mind, body and feelings become one great chorus to God. It is an inner

15

praying which expresses the intimate relationship of love to the heavenly Father. It is a praying of one's spirit with the Spirit of God (Rom. 8.16). It is a praying that floods over one's being in which one finds God has kindled a small flame within. It is beyond the range where words are adequate. It is in the area where the mere placing of thoughts into rational categories is insufficient.

This is the prayer of the heart which is more given by God than produced by us, except in our receptivity and expectant awareness of God's presence. It is the inner prayer of merely living in God's presence, a prayer that can be 'prayed' anytime and anyplace. As such it becomes the prayer 'without ceasing' (1 Thess. 5.17, KJV). Dimitri of Rostov, one of the most celebrated preachers in the history of the Russian Orthodox Church, said: 'All that is necessary is to raise your mind to God, and descend deep into yourself, and this can be done everywhere.'[10]

The call to discover God's deepening presence stands in a dynamic relationship to our call to wholeness. Only as we are truly free can we be free of 'every weight, and sin which clings so closely' (Heb. 12.1, RSV) and which keeps us from discovering the depths of a life lived in Christ.

The third movement of the inner work of God, lastly, is done through the building of I-Thou relationships. We do not deepen our lives in the mysteries of God in order to escape people, but to discover them at the deepest level of our relationships to them. Merton affirmed that the mystery of the discovery of the true self in us is that, 'I must look for my identity, somehow, not only in God but in other men. I will never be able to find myself if I isolate myself from the rest of mankind as if I were a different kind of being.'[11]

Jesus spent a great deal of His time with the twelve dealing with the matter of interpersonal relationships. How were they to relate to each other and to other persons outside of the circle? They came asking, 'Who is going to be the greatest in the Kingdom?' 'Can I sit at your right hand when you come into your glory?' 'There are those who are casting out demons in your name, but they don't belong to our group!' 'Who is my neighbour?'

Martin Buber pointed out that when we treat each other as an it-object we have done something to ourselves as well as others. We have dehumanized each other and taken away the recognition of the other as a creation made in the image of God.

Our world is full of such it-relationships with other persons. Out of our having sufficiently dealt with our true selves, we can begin to know each other as authentic selves also. Likewise, we really cannot know ourselves fully unless we have each other. As you tell me who I am, I begin to have a more complete picture of my true self. Also out of experiencing the love of God through a deeper relationship with you, I grow to understand the beauty of my relationship with God.

Once again, the three dimensions of the inner work of God are dynamic in the uncovering of the true self, the self made in God's image. God works with us through His call to wholeness, the deepening of our relationship with Him and with others. He tugs the inner cords of our lives into deeper and deeper areas of Christian growth.

Meditation Exercises

This week you begin your daily time of meditative reflection as part of the growth process involved in working with this book. Your first assignment is to work meditatively with Psalm 139. This is one way of allowing God to do His work deeply enough to allow the true self to begin to emerge.

The work of meditation is a discipline and requires certain skills.[12] It is not difficult, but as you first try to do it, you may find your resistances beginning to surface. Stay with this discipline and gradually the process will begin to yield to you its fruit, and the depths of the Scriptures will begin to unfold themselves to you in ways no Bible commentary will ever be able to speak to you. Involved will be the interfacing of the pilgrimage of God's people, as recorded in the Scriptures, with your life's pilgrimage. As you allow this dialogue to take place within you, the power of the Scriptures will be released within you at a new depth.

Meditation on the Scriptures has two goals. First of all, it teaches you how to withdraw yourself, even in the midst of busy exterior activities, and to get below the surface of life. Second, it teaches you how to become aware of the presence of God in areas of daily living, where normally you have not been looking for God's activity. All of this is directed toward the development of a life-style of 'constant loving attention to God and dependence on him' and an allowing of your true self to emerge.

Let five *P*'s guide you in your meditative process.[13]

First PREPARE. Prepare a place where you will not be disturbed: a room in your home, the sanctuary in the church, any place where you will not be disturbed for a period of time. Prepare yourself by stilling your mind and your body so that all the straining, worries, and preoccupations of the day are momentarily left behind, outside the door. Prepare yourself to sit in expectant awareness of God's presence in your midst, the expectancy of God's voice being heard by you at a deep level of your being. Open your Bible to Psalm 139, so that as the stillness, the silence, and inner readiness are prepared, you will not have to be distracted by having to look for a Bible and then to locate the passage.

PICTURE the passage as you read it. Picture the God who is constantly aware of you. Picture God's knowing you so deeply that, as a lover, He can anticipate your every word, your every mood, your every action, even before you know that movement yourself. Picture your own attempt to flee from that Presence and the futility of it, for there is no place to escape from His deep penetrating knowledge of you. Picture yourself known by God, even in your mother's womb. Picture the awe and mystery of God's capacity to know you. Begin to picture your own love and adoration at this tender, loving affection He shows toward you in His knowledge of you. Finally, picture yourself asking God to know you even more than He has in the past and to help you know yourself as He knows you, so that you may follow His slightest footstep day by day.

PONDER, turn over and over in your mind and heart, the meaning of God's knowing you that deeply. Allow this to be the time when you humbly stand in expectant awareness of God's speaking to you *His* message from the Scriptures this day. Ask, Jesus, what do you have to say to me through this passage?

PRAY. This is your part of the conversation. Tell God how you are feeling, where the comforts and discomforts of the day are speaking to you. Talk to Him as you would any person standing in the room beside you. If it helps, place an empty chair in front of you, and make your conversation to the 'unseen guest' who occupies it.

PROMISE out of your conversation that which seems to speak to you at the deepest level of your life today. You may simply say, 'As a result of this conversation today, I promise . . .'

Work only with a section of the Psalm at a time. Do not attempt to work deeply with the entire Psalm at one time. Let its message work gradually with you over the entire week. Four or five verses at a time usually are enough to work deeply with each day. As you work with this Psalm each day, gradually you will find those verses coming back to you over and over during the day. This is how you begin to develop skills of awareness of God's Presence at times other than during your meditations.

2

As a Flower Opens to the Sun

We suffer from trying to do God's work. We programme it, schedule it, work up all kinds of goals, aims, objectives, and strategies. Then we get under the weight of those plans and become very task-directed. Everything exists and happens around those plans. Neither looking right nor left, all of our visions and energies are focused on those tasks which have to be accomplished. People, other events, interruptions, become obstacles to the task before us.

I've lived that way for much of my life, and yet I knew that there existed a whisper within me which said, *There is another way*. For me, I never seemed to be available to that other way until I met Jack. Jack is a plumber and an active layman in his church. He called me up one day and asked me to have lunch with him. He wanted to talk about a project he was working on.

As we started to eat our lunch, I asked Jack what kind of things had been recently happening to him. He began to tell me of a ministry to the city jail, a work he was doing in a home he had helped start for unwed mothers, a laymen's retreat programme he led once a month, and an intense study programme he was undertaking to prepare himself for some new work within his church. Then he tried to enlist me in helping him start two more projects! I responded, 'Hey, hold on! I can't even keep up with all you've got going now. How in the world do you do it?' His answer was simply, 'No pain, no strain—it just flows.'

I think for many of us that is a difficult answer to hear. We

20

are straining to get God's work done, rather than discovering another way to be involved. Now I am not saying that doing all of those things Jack was doing is what any one of us should be doing. Maybe that's too much activity for anyone. But I really felt that he was in touch with the Source from which all of life flows, something that I needed to know about.

Many persons have plainly described that dimension of life in terms of availability. In Italian, it is called *disponibilità*, or the holding of oneself or anything in readiness until it is called for. With a bank, for example, the deposits are said to be held 'available', or on call.[1]

When we hold ourselves *available* to God, we release ourselves from the strain of 'making things happen *for* God', which is all too descriptive of much of our religious activity today. Instead, what is needed is a depth of activity which may be described as 'co-operating with grace'. What results is a relaxedness that may seem to some as not being concerned enough because there is no aggressiveness about what needs to be done. The person who has learned to live life available to God at this deeper level allows available human energy to co-operate with divine power in the accomplishment of desired ends.

Availability involves three things. First of all, it includes a receptivity to God that means we are truly present to Him. Too much of the time we simply are not really present to God. We are just not all there. Much of us is elsewhere, and consequently, we are completely unaware of God's activity around and in us, in and through others, and in and through events.

This kind of presence involves our whole beings in much the same way as a golfer is said to concentrate on hitting the ball so much that the slightest whisper, noise, or movement becomes an annoying distraction which may cost the game. However, our presence to God is not a straining presence, as if we were trying to push and force our whole being to be present. It is the relaxed, total awareness of a blind person who, no longer depending on eyes, has tuned every other receptor of his body to such a fine awareness that messages which sighted persons never become aware of are heard on what seems to be a different wavelength. The movement of air which is produced when a person walks by goes unnoticed by most of us, for we are not dependent on that sense for our information. But messages are there that could be read, and are read, by the non-sighted person through skin sensations, hearing, smell, and taste. We who are sighted have the same capacities for using these message receivers, but do not. And, in a real sense, we are not as truly present to a situation.

Being truly present also involves our minds. Because our minds are capable of much more rapid movement than it takes our eyes to read, or our ears to hear one speak, we are capable of inattention to persons as they speak. We merely are not listening. We hear most of what is said, enough to fill in the blanks of what we miss. But we are also capable of fixing our car or watching a show on television while we listen to each other or even listening to two conversations at one time. Because we do this, we do not concentrate all of our mental abilities to listening to what the other is saying.

When we do not have all of our sensory receivers working, and our minds are shuttling between the person's words and something else, we just are not deeply present to each other. This is tragic, whether it involves persons, events, or our relationship to God. It means that we tend to treat these as things rather than as instruments of God's communication to us. We do not see all the significance of an event. We miss the importance of a person's relationship to us. God's activity goes on all around us, and we are tragically unaware of it.

Douglas Steere, known to many as a respected teacher of the life of prayer, in commenting on how Søren Kierkegaard viewed listening, said that in any religious service there are three persons present: the listener, the speaker, and God.[2] Too often the listener assumes a totally detached, critical stance toward the message, both in terms of the content and the style of delivery. Instead of doing that, Kierkegaard said that the listener needs to see himself on the platform talking, with God listening, and the original speaker simply standing in the wings as an old-time theatrical prompter. He felt that in our listening process we need to enter into the process of another at a deeper level if we are to say that we truly listened.

In a similar manner, the translator of Martin Buber's classic, *I and Thou*, said that the translator of Buber needed to get inside the original writer and see and think as he did.[3] Only then would the translation speak as the author had spoken in the original language. Instead, when the translator's message interfered, it became an attempt to pass off the translator's ideas as those of the author. Even Buber, when he translated the Old Testament into German, tried to go beyond the superficial work of most translations which were done merely by associating the root meaning of one word with the root meaning of another. Instead, Buber sought to saturate himself in early Jewish thought process *before* he proceeded with the translation.

Malcolm Muggeridge, in a book about the work of Mother Teresa of Calcutta, said that what seemed so startling about the work of Mother Teresa and her fellow workers among the thousands of Calcutta's wretched, is that *she is totally present to every human being*.[4] Every baby discarded in a garbage can, every dying person, every leper, every derelict is a human being worthy of her undivided attention. The loving care and total presence to the poor have caused her to be acknowledged as one of today's living saints.

To be available, we must be truly present with all of our beings in a loving attention to events, persons, and the inner voice of God. Being available is a stilling of our restlessness, found in our constant moving from one thing to another, so that we may be present to the *now*. We must be attentive to the one who is with us *now*, the event that is happening *now*, to God's voice *now*. Being available is a gentle, relaxed awareness of all that is going on around us in *this* moment. We must listen to what is beyond the words and see the intent of those words, hearing the intended message. In order for one to be available to God's slightest whisper, one must come to that stillness which means that she is truly present to His voice.

A second ingredient of availability is gentleness.[5] I once saw a full-page ad in a newspaper for a best-selling book which claimed to teach people how to be successful through intimidation. According to the ad, all one had to do to win was to intimidate one's opponent. This view says that people are basically adversaries. Because an adversarial relationship is inevitable, according to this philosophy, persons might as well learn how to function in that kind of situation.

This view certainly is a stark contrast to the Jesus of whom Isaiah and Matthew spoke:

> He will not argue or shout,
>   or make loud speeches in the streets.
> He will be gentle to those who are weak,
>   and kind to those who are helpless.
> He will persist until he causes justice to triumph.
>   (Matt. 12.19–20, GNB)

A tense, angry, strained person breaks reeds that have already been weakened and snuffs out the little fire left in a smouldering wick.

Crash the door down! Break open the gates! Take charge, even if you have to get tough! This is certainly different from a style of 'expectant awareness' to God's presence which allows a gentleness within us to take hold and wait.

The psalmist said, 'The humble will possess the land and enjoy prosperity and peace' (Ps. 37.11, GNB). Jesus said to the disciples, 'How blest are those of a gentle spirit; they shall have the earth for their possession' (Matt. 5.5, NEB).

For many the word *gentle* has lost all of the impact of its meaning. For many it means being a sissy, a wimp, Mr Casper Milquetoast, or a wallflower, Miss Penelope Pipsqueak. Gentleness, however, has to do with one's inner aggressiveness which does not allow one to be truly available to each person, each event, and to God. One takes those persons and events and works with an aggressive spirit on them, so that they no longer yield up their true selves, only the defensive reactions that seek to protect themselves from our rough interruption into their existence. When that happens no longer are we dialoguing with the real person or event but with their defence structures. The real person, or the real event, remains hidden behind the barricades that have hastily been set up as a defence against our intrusions.

However, when we treat each person, each event, with the gentleness that allows that person or event to yield up its own meaning for that particular moment, we have experienced the depths of that individual or experience. No longer do we have to impose our meanings, our wills, our viewpoints on each person or occasion. We have not broken the bruised reed, nor snuffed out the last, smouldering flicker of the fire of hope.

We all know the gentleness of handling a newborn baby, the overprotectiveness for a sick child, the hand on a fevered head, the soft caresses of two lovers, the care and attention of a person involved in an accident. What we experience is the vulnerability of the other, the fragility of the person or the moment. So we approach the person or the event with a gentleness that respects that vulnerability.

A man once translated for me that Beatitude which reads,

'Blessed are the meek' as 'Blessed are those who don't go around kicking in people's doors!' Gentleness doesn't have to kick in the door of another person's life, or the door of any event. And when we don't, that person or that event is available to us in a way that, when we act out of our inner aggressiveness, doesn't allow us to be fully present. The gentle person is more fully present to persons and events than the person who acts out of inner aggressiveness. She is a person who is able to hear more deeply all that a person or event has to say.

Gentleness doesn't allow a harshness to enter into our relationships with each other. The other person becomes very special to us, and we approach that one with a softness that speaks of our deep appreciation of him. Even when harshness is present in that one's life, and doesn't allow him to be gentle with us, our vulnerability allows gentleness to be restored in him.

Finally, gentleness affects our relationship and availability towards God's presence. We do not demand that He come and do for us now. When we come into His presence with gentleness, our attitude about His comings and goings in our lives is not one of command, but a gentle receptivity to His times of presence as well as His times of seeming absence. God does not come and go at our bidding. The gentleness of our hearts helps us to be aware of His footsteps so that our availability to do His good pleasure is increased. As a result, it becomes much easier to pray and meditate on His word, for we do not approach Him demandingly but with an openness to hear His fresh word for our lives.

The third element in availability is an inward attentiveness. This is an at-oneness with God at a deep level of awareness. It is a listening with patience and without the need for a great deal of talking. Some would call this inward attentiveness a sensitivity to the faintest whisper of God.

Others have described it as a willingness to live life out of the nudgings of the Holy Spirit.

Such willingness is like being a sensitive instrument acutely tuned to the inward frequency of God's Holy Spirit. It is being truly present and gentle. A person who is present with the Holy Spirit is willing to risk acting on the slightest nudging of that needle whereby we sense that God would have us be here or there, do this or that.

Have you ever experienced being drawn to someone, even though large distances separated you? or felt that God had laid a certain person or burden on your heart? It may have happened in a time of prayer, meditation, or quiet reflection that a certain person came to your mind and stayed there for a time. Have you ever experienced the sudden impulse to speak to a person about a matter, share an insight, affirm a gift that the person was not aware of, or ask for help from a person? In many of these and other ways, the Holy Spirit uses the sensitivity of a human being, who has been prepared through an inward attentiveness, to carry the message, the ministry of affirmation to another, or even to receive the ministry of another.

The risk of being available comes not just in being truly present to a person, and in being gentle, but especially at the point of inward attentiveness. As we begin to be nudged, we risk being misunderstood, being thought of as some odd nut, or being labelled a fanatic. But the New Testament account seems to say that part of the fantastic power of the witness of the early Christians came through their ministry of just being available at the right time, to the right persons, in the right places. They were attuned to God as a flower opens to the sun.

Meditation Exercises

This week the meditative experience will focus on three events in the Book of Acts. Each event tells the story of a person who was available at the right time for the work of the Lord. The Holy Spirit in each case was the evangelist, and the work of evangelism was done by Him. But human instrumentality was present to the activity of the Holy Spirit and, through an inward gentleness and attentiveness, co-operated with God in a significant action. Where we are so accustomed to 'making it happen', in none of these three cases did human causal factors make it happen. But in each case there was human co-operation with grace. This is the ministry of availability.

Work with *each one of the following passages* for *two days* or stay with the single passage all week,
— Acts 8.26–40, the availability of Philip
— Acts 9.10–19, the availability of Ananias
— Acts 10.1–33, 44–48, the availability of Peter

As you read each passage, try to place yourself at the event. Smell the smells, hear the sounds, experience everything about the incidents that are taking place. Then answer the following questions as you seek to get below the surface of the words in the passages:

1. Name that which the individual was asked to do by the Holy Spirit.

2. In what way do you know that the person was 'available' to the leadership of the Holy Spirit for that particular task?

3. Name the *obstacle* that each had to overcome in order to be available (for example, Philip, a layman, was sent to instruct a learned government official in the meaning of a biblical text).

4. What was the personal *risk* that was involved in being available (for example, Ananias risked healing the man who could have had him arrested for being part of the illegal religious group).

5. Using a *colour* to represent that person's feelings at the

risk involved, describe how you think that person felt (for example, red might represent anger, or orange, fear).

So far you have tried to get behind the words of the biblical account to understand and feel how another handled the ministry of availability. Now bring this meditation closer to your life with one final question.

6. What keeps you from being available to the nudgings of God's Holy Spirit in a daily ministry and witness wherever you are?

As you work with each of the three passages, begin to ask yourself, 'How can I become more available to persons and events through an in-tuneness with God?'

Name three areas of your life where you are going to try to be more available this week.

3

Letting Go My 'Isaacs'

You will never find the depths of availability open to you until you make some conscious effort to deliver yourself up in 'holy abandonment' to God's activity in, through, and around you. This is the first work of preparation, God's inner work within you as He seeks to draw you into a deeper way of living, open to His slightest whisper. Abandonment, prayer, and a daily quiet time in which you 'waste time for God' become preparations for this deeper dialogue during each moment of our day. It is God's work within you, the preparation for a more transcendent life-style, built on the emergence of the true self-in-Christ.

The first preparation for this deeper living is abandonment, a foundational disposition of allowing God's work within to take place on His terms. His activity in us may not be understood, in spite of the acuteness of all the rational categories we have fashioned, all of the impulses we have to do good, and all the right motivations for action which come to us. But there must be a foundational 'letting go' process of abandonment to God's good pleasure which allows His work within us to occur at a very deep level.

Abandonment purifies us from the excessive 'managerial hold' we have on every detail of our lives. We like to control our lives, and we live in the illusion that we are guiding and controlling our lives into certain directions. We modify James' advice, 'If it be the Lord's will, we shall live to do this or that' (Jas. 4.15, NEB). We would much rather plan our lives in greater detail and then add on that statement to satisfy all the requirements. We don't like to turn loose, let go, open our hands to receive as the heavenly Father wishes to give.

Overly aggressive willfulness is the squeezing of every experience to make it fit into the patterns in which we allow our lives to be lived. All of life, every person and event, must fit the rigid, predetermined mould we have set for life, or not at all. It is a pushing of everything around us to move toward conformity. It is taking charge of all events in our lives so that they are directed toward certain predetermined ends. We become upset with less than perfect outcomes for every experience. We become rigid, brittle, and all of life is one big pattern that is seen only by us. Every event and person has to be calculated, sized up, and evaluated before we allow it to be ours.

Control becomes the name of the game—otherwise, we are afraid that things will get out of hand. We control the conversation, the activity, the people we are around, how close they can get to us, and we to them. We feel more adequate if we can control the situation. We know the game, so we make the rules. If we break them, we no longer play.

Really, we use control as an inward mechanism to cope with anxieties. We are such tense persons that even our bodies, muscles, and endocrine glands tell everyone how tense we are. But we feel better if the game is played within certain boundaries. And when there is an unknown area, we rehearse the scene five, six, or even ten times, *before* we get involved. We rehearse all the time: what we will say, what she will say, what we will answer, and how she will reply. We watch ourselves walk in, and go over it over and over again until we get the movements down just right. People think we walk and talk like wooden soldiers; that is the only way we can get through it. Otherwise, we feel very exposed, in plain sight for everyone to see, and with no place to hide. It is safer that way, more protected, less vulnerable.

Overly aggressive willfulness and control are two ways you

and I manage our inner tensions and anxieties when we are asked to just let go and be more open to each moment of God's creation. The writers of the spiritual classics have described abandonment as that openness to the loving care of the Father in each moment. In the words of Jesus, 'Your Father knows what you need before you ask him' (Matt. 6.8, RSV). At the deepest level of relationship, we expose our weakness (finitude) to the care of the Father. Abandonment is a vulnerability to life, believing that the Father knows our needs, our capacities, and the direction in which our lives should go, even better than we do.

Vulnerability is found in our behaviour by being open and receptive to the Father's working out of events in our lives. It is an attempt to stop rehearsing each scene, as if all of life depended on that moment. It is an attempt to stop riding through life with the brakes on. It is an inward releasing of the controls so that a spontaneity of our total person can be available to every experience we encounter. It is learning to make the leaps of faith without signposts and diagrams that echo with Jesus, 'Not as I will, but as thou wilt' (Matt. 26.39, KJV).

Too often we are signpost, or diagram, Christians. We will follow God's will *if* He will show us the way. 'Wherever He leads I'll go'—if He will just show me the way *before* I have to walk it! We can follow signposts or mileage indicators on the highway and know which way we are going and exactly where we are in relationship to the next town. Or we can read a diagram and tell where everything is supposed to be. But it touches us too deeply to have to travel along with no signposts or diagrams to follow.

We really don't like wandering in the desert for forty years. That is too much. Yet the journey we are on more often than not demands that we place our hands in God's hands and start out. The commentary by the writer of the Book of Hebrews, after having sung the praises of many Old Testament heroes of faith, was 'All of these died in faith, before receiving any of the things that had been promised, but they saw them in the far distance and welcomed them, recognising that they were only *strangers and nomads on earth*' (Heb. 11.13, JB).

The journey is one of turning loose in order to follow, even if the path is through darkness, dryness, pain, anguish, inner helplessness, personal anxiety, and inadequacy. In each of these, God's loving care is guiding us toward His perfect will in us, if we can but learn greater dependence on Him, an abandonment in all things.

We do not have to initiate all the activity of our lives, even the activity of our religious existence. We do not have to will all that happens to us. God's activity is at work in us, around us, and through us, if we can learn that obedience of co-operating with His activity. We really want to live in and through the Lord in a more relaxed movement of our lives that is characterized by freedom, openness, spontaneity, and creativity. But what is the resistance that we feel deep down within us? Is it the fear and anxiety of letting go of the controls of our lives? Is it the fear that if we 'let go' somehow everything about us will fly to pieces?

We learn early in life to anticipate persons, events, and even God. We learn that this is one way we can control what happens around us and to us. If we can anticipate another's thoughts or actions, we can plan our own strategy of response. With God we look and look at the past in order to try to predict how the future will turn out. This is a way of anticipating how God will work in us. By doing this, we 'permit' God's activity in the future to be only experienced in those categories in which we have cast the past.

We even plot the future through possibilities. We create possible futures and then begin to pick and choose which would be more advantageous. In so doing, we try to anticipate God, even 'helping God out' just a little bit as we see one scenario beginning to take place. We make two or three phone calls, or write a letter or two to just the right friends, so God won't have to work too hard in making that possible future come about! We justify ourselves by saying, 'God helps those who help themselves.'

Another issue in abandonment to God's activity in and through us is the relinquishing of undue anticipation. An overly anxious anticipation of all the events of one's life is a life lived for the most part in the future, unaware of the activity of God in the present moment. When we do that, we say that the future is in God's hands *but* accomplished by *our power*. We attempt to make the future dependent on our physical and intellectual power *alone* without a recognition of God's activity, protection, and guidance.

One of the most difficult dimensions of the spiritual life (a life that is Holy Spirit-directed) is to understand the inter-relationship of our efforts and the work of God. Abandonment is not the resignation of a whipped dog, nor is it an acquiescence to something beyond our control. It is not just sheer conformity to a plan that is imposed without involvement of one's will. It is not simply going limp in a resignation to a superior power. Abandonment goes much deeper.

Abandonment is a holy indifference, a setting oneself at the disposition of God. It is a spirit of allowing—a child-like leap across the empty space into the loving arms of the Father. Abandonment is a surrendering of our lives to be pliable to the co-creative work of the Father. It is neither an acquiescence in which we give up total responsibility for our lives nor an aggressive willfulness in which we take charge of all that happens in and around us. It is being totally receptive to God's activity through a loving openness on our part, and then joining with God in the activity of His will.

The will of God for our lives is not some external force that we have to accept in a submissive act of obedience. God's good pleasure is that we seek the fullest possibilities for our lives and for the world in which we live. He knows that certain things in our lives, and in the world, are chains which bind us and cause less of ourselves to be known. God's good pleasure is really an 'interior invitation of personal love'.

Too often we see God's will as the 'arbitrary dictates of a domineering and insensible Father'.[1] These are more often seeds of hatred within us which obscure our vision of God who has our deepest interest at heart. And, when we make of God's will an 'arbitrary force bearing down upon us with implacable hostility',[2] it drives us to despair. Much of our viewpoint of God will determine how we see God's good pleasure for us.

'I wish I knew what I am supposed to do,' is often heard, as if God has not given us freedom through the choices that are available. As we face each moment and each event in life, God gives us freedom to choose. In those moments, we experience the freedom that God has given us children. In most situations, no *one thing* will be acceptable, but many are God's good pleasure. As choices become ours, we are given the opportunity of becoming co-creators with God in the working out of our true identity.

Too often we simply resign ourselves to events and say, 'Well, that's the way it was meant to be.' Both this and the former statement bear with them the seed of a viewpoint which says that somehow God has all possible choices worked out in a master plan in the sky and that He plays games with mortals by tormenting them with, 'Which choice is the right choice?' Then He slaps our hands when we get the wrong one. Or when tragedy, sickness, or a reversal of our plans happens, we simply give up to a game plan that God's 'great computer in the sky' had worked out for us and ours is only the choice of being resigned to it.

If these were the ways God's will was worked out, then our lives would have to be based on resignation, submission, acquiescence, or conformity to it. Ours would be an existence of oughts, shoulds, and have-tos. There would be no freedom to be, no freedom to become co-creators with God in the ongoing creation in me and in the world around me.

But that is not the case. *Abandonment* means to be in dialogue in depth with God's purposes and to co-operate with God's activity. When we are co-operating with God, a little effort goes a long way. When we are not, no matter how much effort we expend, we never seem to be able to accomplish those things that we've set out to do. If God's purposes were to achieve a forced submission to a rigid will, then there would be no room for a person of faith. Instead God, through an inner sensing of His presence, a hunger for His presence, draws us to Himself in an inner abandonment. This abandonment leaps across the reasonable boundaries of human existence to rest in an attitude of allowing, in which we become aware of God's hidden activity in each experience and in each moment. Then, we ask not to see the plan or the road map. We just rest in the assurance that the step we are taking now is also His will.

Our effort is necessary for God's good pleasure to be worked out in our lives and through us in the world. Always that which we must be sensitive to is when we are exerting too much effort and, therefore, are not totally indifferent to what God is asking of us, and have begun to do 'religious, busy work' out of an overly aggressive willfulness. Likewise, we need to be sensitive to those times when we know what God's good pleasure is, but refuse to act on it by saying, 'I will wait on God.' The spiritual writers knew this as the heresy of 'quietism'. Do absolutely nothing, just sit with an empty mind, heart, and senses and wait. This is not likely to be the sin of our modern Christianity, which too often urges its faithful on to 'do something, even if it's wrong!'

The balance, said Thomas Merton, is to be found in two words, *obedience* and *abandonment*.

> Ultimately the secret of all this is perfect abandonment to the will of God in things you cannot control, and perfect obedience to Him in everything that depends on your own volition, so that in all things, in your interior life and in your outward works of God, you desire only one thing, which is the fulfillment of His will.[3]

Therefore, in obedience to what we have understood to be God's good pleasure for us and our lives, and our actions of co-creation with Him, we continue to do what we are doing as we have understood it the last time the Father indicated a particular direction for our lives. We don't need to ask each day if some action should be performed. We do what we earlier discerned to be God's direction for us. We develop a certain sensitivity that allows us to be flexible to the interruptions and unscheduled events of the day, so we see these as unscheduled opportunities which God sends our way. But obedience is a part of our living. And with it the prayer of Thomas à Kempis becomes ours: 'Grant that I may be one with you in choosing and in rejecting, that I may be unable to choose or reject except as you would do.'[4]

Abandonment, both in the midst of obedience as an inward disposition and during those times when events and circumstances are happening to us and around us for which we have no control, is to pray the prayer of Merton:

> My Lord God, I have no idea where I am going. I do not see the road ahead of me. I cannot know for certain where it will end. Nor do I really know myself, and the fact that I think I am following your will does not mean that I am actually doing so. But I believe that the desire to please you does in fact please you. AMEN.[5]

In the midst of darkness, while the fog covers our understanding, abandonment may mean just standing still until the fog lifts—a waiting, not of the quietist, but of expectant awareness which is not straining, but with keen anticipation knows that God's activity is in the fog and darkness, also.

An inward detachment from desires, cares, worries, anxieties, and anything else that keeps us from being free to be attuned to God's will is necessary if we attain that abandonment of living which allows us to live at the deepest level of our true selves. If we are bound by the constant changing desires, feelings, and impulses within us, we will not be able to be free, open, and available to God's divine purposes. Detachment is an important ingredient of what it means to abandon one's self to God's holy will.

Detachment implies not being unduly influenced by anything that we love and desire for its own sake. When that happens, no longer can we see the choices that have to be made from the vantage of freedom. Those things begin to influence the way we choose, so that they begin to determine for us God's will. They destroy our moral judgement and our sense of valuing. No longer do we see with the clarity of abandonment what God is saying to us. There have arisen hidden attachments to this or that which begin to influence and persuade within us the choices that we make. We find ourselves governed by acquired tastes, habits, and wish-dreams. Sometimes these motivators of our behaviour are within reach of our conscious awareness, but more often they lie below the surface of our conscious existence and, therefore, are inaccessible to us as the real stimulators of our conduct unless in transcendent reflection we seek them out with God's grace.

Abandonment, then, involves a detachment from those things which may hinder our freely hearing the slightest whisper of God. It involves more than a temperate use of things, for it calls us to a death to that which hinders our availability to the God who says, 'Now it is time to move on.' Unconscious forms of attachment are examined and allowed to be pried loose from their clinging hold on us. It may involve the slowing down of life, so that we no longer grasp on to the sound of a radio, the inane entertainment of the television, or the senseless rounds of entertaining which go under the name of 'being together'. It will mean the development of an inner freedom that can allow us to wrestle with the deepest meaning of God's activity in and around us. It is a trusting in the events and circumstances of life, not as gifts from a hostile environment, but sent for the good of my life. We are able to penetrate into the deepest meanings of events and persons because we are free from those attachments which seem momentarily to be the very essence of our existence. We are able to perceive God's activity as we turn loose in holy abandonment.

Meditation Exercises

This week during your meditation time, work with the incident of Abraham going out to sacrifice Isaac. This is a story of abandonment.

The story examines the powerful inner tugs of abandonment. The Bible was written by persons familiar with the interior landscape of their lives and has to be understood by those willing to make that same pilgrimage and lay their Bible alongside their own pilgrimage and allow God to speak to them about their own costly abandonments.

Use the Scripture passage, Genesis 22.1–18, as the basis for your meditations this week. If you need to gain some background for the story read: Genesis 12.1–3; 15.1–6; 16.1–16; 17.15–20; 18.9–15; and 21.1–7. Use the process suggested in chapter 1 for the first three days of your meditations.

Days 1–3—Prepare, picture, ponder, pray, and promise.

Day 4—On the fourth day, instead of picturing, place yourself in the role of Abraham and write out a *dialogue* between you and God. Place your name on the first line, then God's name on the second line. Write out by your name what you would say to God about this request to sacrifice your son. Then write God's response. This requires your imagination, but allow this imaginary dialogue to go on as long as the conversation continues to flow, first your words, then God's.

At some point the dialogue will stop. Don't force it, but allow it to continue as long as it will. Writing out this conversation will allow you to see a progression. At first it will seem strange to write down 'He said' and 'I said', but it will help you to sense the conversation between you (Abraham) and God about this act of abandonment. Argue with God, question Him in any direction, allow yourself to become involved; discuss this thing that God has asked you to do. After you have written the conversation, allow it to be the basis for your pondering and praying and promising for this day.

Days 5–6—For the last two days of this week allow your meditations to be focused around this anonymously written meditation and work with the questions which follow.

And Everyone Has His Own Isaac[6]

I want Abraham for my friend, said God.
I would make him a people great,
    more than the sea-sands, a people
    and a new land
    and a blessing.
I will give him Isaac, said God.

And Abraham, looking up, loved back.
I will build altars in the land you gave me, friend.
    an altar at Sichem
    an altar at Valley of Clear Seeing.
      Move on.

an altar east of Bethel, west of Hai.
So Abram built the altars.

And Abram moved his tent by Mamre
at Hebron built an altar to the Lord.

Then God took Abram out of doors,
My childless friend, said God,
Look up at the countless stars.
And God said,
Abram, I am going to pluck a son from you,
a son to give you sons.
You'll have more sons than stars, said God,
before we're through.

So Abram put his faith in God
and it was reckoned virtue.

But God left Abram waiting,
Gave him time
Time almost to count the stars.

But one day God called Abram, remembering the stars, and said,
Abram, you shall have a new name.
And God called him, 'Father of many Nations'
God, taunting, called him Abraham.

And friends have covenants, said God,
and we will have one too, He said.
I am your God and you are my own Abraham.
The sign is in your flesh.

Later God thought:
I cannot leave him counting stars forever.
Already Sara laughs at me.
It is time.
It is time I gave him Isaac, said God.

And Abraham became the father of a son, Isaac.
A hundred years of unspent fatherhood
he poured all out on Isaac.
And laughing Sara's breasts grew warm and full.
Themselves they gave to Isaac.

There was no more counting stars for God's poor friend.
He had the seed for all the flowers of earth.
God had given Abraham his Isaac.

And God watched Abraham with love.
Watched him as he played with sheep and land.
And later on, He spoke:

I am the Pack-Rat God, said God.
and now, Abraham,
I want Isaac.

But we are friends and you gave Isaac, Abr'am said,

I know we are, said God.
But I want Isaac.

Till Abr'am cried,
The stars so countless and the many sands
and would you take my one son Isaac?

And God would only answer back:
I want Isaac.

And Abraham, because he was a friend of God's
    said, God,
        Take Isaac.

1. Where do I sense God's activity in my life that threatens
   me?
2. Where am I controlling and anxious?
3. Where do I cling to the very existence of life?
4. How would I experience a kind of 'death' if I were to let go
   of ——————— and abandon myself to God's good
   pleasure?
5. What might happen in my life if I really turned loose?

4

God Alone

Inscribed in the stone above the doorway that leads into the retreat house at the Abbey of Gethsemani near Louisville, Kentucky, are two words: 'God Alone'. They signify the deep work of prayer in silence and solitude. In an ever-deepening openness to God, the second movement of God's inner preparation in us is an allowing of prayer to become a relationship in which we learn to rest in the Lord.

As pilgrims who only understand where we've been as we look backward, prayer becomes the daily conversation necessary if we are to be available to God's activity in each moment. Prayer becomes the dialogue between two who are seeking to bring together 'all things in Christ, things in heaven and things on earth' (Eph. 1.10). In order to join with God in a ministry of reconciliation, there must be a parallel deepening of our lives of conversation with the heavenly Father. The peril of activism in our Western Christianity finds its counterpart in how we pray. We want to be busy *doing* instead of *knowing* at a deep level whether the activity of our busyness is in harmony with the Father's good pleasure.

Our difficulty in any serious prayer life today is found in our inability to slow down the pace of life, as well as in some serious misconcepts about prayer itself. Time that is not filled with some activity is considered inactivity. And we have had too many lectures in our childhood, which have been later reinforced in the adult culture, that lead us to believe that life is to be measured in what we do and how much we *have* after we have done it. These are found in questions which we pose to each other, such as, 'What did you do last night?' 'What do you do [meaning what business or occupation are you in]?' 'How much did you get?' 'Where are you going?'

Any serious personal relationship costs time and involvement. A passing acquaintance with others is not very costly. That is the kind of relationship we have with the clerk in the store, the persons who bring the paper and the mail, the employees in the other departments from the one we work in. We have many of these superficial relationships with people, and this probably has to be the case in a complex and urban society such as ours. But superficial relationships are not adequate between husband and wife, between parent and children, between close friends. Those relationships cost time and presence.

So it is with God. Prayer is the language of relationship between us and God. It can be very superficial so that we just 'ring Him up' when we need Him, or as we mumble the prayer that we learned as children a couple of times a week. Or prayer can be the serious relationship between us and our Heavenly Father, which was demonstrated by Jesus in the Model Prayer (Matt. 6.9–13). In that prayer He showed us a relationship of acknowledgment of God as Father, a revering of God as the Holy Other, a recognition that we desire that God's good pleasure be continually having sway on earth, a recognition of dependence daily for food and other necessities, a request for forgiveness and an acknowledgment that we will forgive as we have been forgiven, a petition for not being tempted beyond our endurance, and a final request of salvation from the evil around us. That is a conversation which speaks of a very serious relationship.

Since prayer is primarily a relationship, three misconceptions have to be dealt with. First, prayer is not just another religious activity. Too many of us deal with prayer as something else that has to be done if we are going to be good church members, or at least if we do all the things that Christians are supposed to do. It helps us be in good standing with God, the church, or the organization we belong to. As another religious duty to perform, like attending the meetings of the church, and tithing our income, we perform it hoping that somehow all of this religious activity has some meaning. And our resistance to praying often is at the point that we have so much to *do* that we just don't see how we have time to do any serious praying. Thus we either end up with a very superficial prayer life, or we suffer with deep guilt feelings every time we get into a discussion in church about prayer.

But we know that if the climate of the discussion in church allows all of those present to be truthful, most would admit that they do not have a very serious prayer life either. True, they say the blessing before meals, often have a prayer before retiring in the evening, or sometime during the early minutes when they get out of bed. And many would acknowledge that when they travel to work in the morning, they think of God, and many others would say they have some time during the morning after all the family members are gone. But a really deep conversation with God is something foreign to most.

Prayer, as only another activity, has been the problem for many. We assume that we pray only when we have formal times of praying. Because we cannot spend time in prayer during the day, we think we have not prayed. We excuse ourselves by saying, 'If I didn't have anything else to do, I would pray. But because I am so busy, I just can't pray.' Then the argument proceeds to talk about whether we value God more than other things, and the end result is a big guilt trip for everyone.

True, we need serious quiet time with God daily and periodic longer times of retreat and reflection. But prayer is more than an act we perform once or twice a day. Paul admonished the Thessalonian Christians to 'pray without ceasing' (1 Thess. 5.17, KJV), but he also said to them, 'if any would not work, neither should he eat' (2 Thess. 3.10, KJV). So, when he wrote to them to pray at all times, he was not advocating idleness and laziness. This command of Paul has troubled Christians of all ages and has been mistakenly understood at various times in Christian history to have meant primarily a life devoted to 'saying prayers'. Although life dedicated to prayer is a legitimate vocation, that vocation does not rest on this verse; nor does this verse imply that all Christians, because they cannot have formal prayers on their lips at all times, cannot enter into a life of praying without ceasing.

Vince Dwyer said, 'Prayer is a person's reponse to God, who reveals Himself from moment to moment.' As one is constantly aware of God at the deepest level of one's being, and is aware of God's activity in and around us, we have the possibility of being in constant dialogue with the Heavenly Father. In each event, each person, every experience of the day, we can have an awareness of God that allows us to get to the reality below the surface and become aware of His ultimate purposes being achieved or blocked. It also implies that His presence with us is as real in the office, factory, school, or home as it is in church. God's activity is going on all around us. As we respond to that activity, a conversation with God, which at times does not require many words, can begin within us.

To be able to achieve this deep conversation, as is true of any relationship of depth, there is a cost, for it means we learn a discipline that affects our entire way of approaching life. It means that prayer becomes a way of living at a deeper level than what we have previously attempted in just saying 'prayers'. It becomes a way of praying without ceasing, rather than another religious activity to be added to our already busy religious activities.

Second, praying is not just rest from activity. 'I would pray if I didn't have so much to do,' becomes the protest of many. 'If I had a job that would allow me plenty of time, I could have a serious prayer life.' Or, maybe the protest of those who abandon the cities of the nation with their crime and violence for a 'pastoral flight' to the rural areas of the nation, 'I would pray if I had a restful surrounding.' By making this argument, many are saying that prayer is opposed to activity. It is true that for most of us not slowing down is one of the most serious hindrances to a serious prayer life, but it should not be assumed that prayer is to be equated with slowing down. Many today are turning to techniques of meditation as a way of easing a rat race type of existence. They have found a genuine means for living life a little deeper than being pulled and tugged by every activity around them. It has helped many to begin to act on their lives, rather than merely react to the day-to-day pulls and tugs.

However, slowing down the mind, slowing down the body, finding a restful refuge in the woods somewhere, centring life deeply within one's self is just the 'vestibule of prayer'. It is nothing more than the getting ready for a serious conversation with the heavenly Father. Persons who have stopped here have stopped short of prayer as they have finally decided to slow life down. Though they have experienced the calming, quieting effect of a life that begins to be lived purposefully, they have just got ready for a serious relationship of prayer. Rest, though necessary for a serious prayer life, is not to be equated with prayer itself. It is just the beginning place.

The need to be 're-collected' or 'centred down' before being able to even hear the voice within, to dip down below the conscious level, or to hear the still small voice of God, has been part of the literature of prayer for centuries.

Rest is necessary for a serious relationship with the Father.

If one's schedule of activities is so hectic and hurried that all of life is lived in the tension of going from one activity to another, or having to so concentrate on work that it consumes her, then serious prayer life is threatened or very nearly impossible. In that case, a slowing down of life is necessary, and that may be such a wrenching of life-styles that it is nearly impossible for that person to 'let go'. But that letting go has to be the starting place for any life of prayer which is seriously begun.

However, the error must not be made which assumes that prayer is rest from activity, so that those who seriously pray are not doing anything else. The real goal of the life of prayer is to be in such a deep dialogue with the heavenly Father *as one is engaged in whatever activity one is involved in*; not just to sit in a state of blankness all day long. It is possible to have a deep conversation with the Father all day, in every moment, if one is willing to slow life down sufficiently; is willing to have a serious quiet time out of which the rest of the day moves; and will listen deeply in expectant awareness to the Father's good pleasure.

Third, prayer remains superficial in our relationship with the Father if it is only a prayer of petition. 'Lord give me this', 'Lord help me out of this difficulty', 'Lord if you will do this for me, then I will certainly do this for you.' Intercessory prayer, or the prayer of petition, can be part of a genuine conversation with God. But if that remains the only conversation, then the relationship begins to dry up, not because that is what God wills, but because that is the only relationship we have allowed.

We have treated God as a thing to be called on in times of crisis or need, but at other times ignored. Rightfully, critics of Christianity and many faithful persons have said this type of relationship is nothing more than 'God-of-the-gaps'. We just fill in those gaps when we have exhausted our go-it-alone resources with a prayer of 'Help!' At other times we handle it on our own. This is next to no relationship at all.

That kind of prayer life leads us into those fruitless eddies of discussion which want to deal with, 'Does God answer prayer?' and 'Does anything happen when I pray—do I cause God to act, or is prayer just changing me?' When prayer is considered as only petition, that becomes our line of questioning, and if those discussions never produce satisfying results within us, it may be that we have been asking the wrong questions.

Prayer as relationship involves conversation, a dialogue between two who have come to know each other at increasingly deeper levels. Thus prayer is the result of an ever-deepening relationship with God. In Him we live and move and exist, and in Him we discover our true selves. Therefore, prayer is knowing ourselves and God at deeper and deeper levels.

Too often we pray in language of the sixteenth and seventeenth century with 'thee, thou, and thine'. Also, we change tone and pitch when we pray, as if in talking to God somehow He understands us only when there is a certain 'stained glass voice' about it.

Three and four hundred years ago, *thee*, *thou*, and *thine* were everyday pronouns that expressed intimacy. At that time, the pronoun *you* was used to express distance between the person speaking and the person spoken to. It was used to address a person of high esteem or a person with whom one was not well acquainted. It was only in an egalitarian climate of later centuries that the distinction between the two pronouns gradually gave way to *you* being used both in the second person singular and plural.

With the use of the same form, *you*, there was no more distinction available between intimate relationships and distant relationships as continues to exist in many European languages. What has happened, then, is that those today who use *thou* to pray to God and *you* for normal conversations, and insist that it is more respectful to address God that way, have completely reversed the situation of the English of the King James Bible. It uses 'thou', 'thee' and 'thine' to speak to God in an intimate fashion. This corresponded more faithfully to the Greek. We have been the ones who do not want to use the intimate pronoun *you* in our prayer life because of our hesitancy to be in intimate conversation with the heavenly Father. That's a strange turn of events! Jesus taught us to address god as 'Daddy' (*Abba*), the most intimate of terms.

Prayer, then, begins with an intimate conversation. It is as intimate and real as with anyone else who is close to us. Prayer verifies that God is immanent in His universe. And as prayer deepens, we learn the other dimension of the paradox of God's relationship to His creation—that He is also transcendent. He is beyond and above His creation.

We soon learn that a deep life of conversation with the Father reveals to us the times when He must teach us His trascendence, as His presence is revealed to us in darkness, dryness, obscurity, and dread. There is in the life of prayer a knowing through unknowing; an awareness that thrusts us out into our nothingness and helplessness. But in all of prayer it is basically a conversation of two intimates at deeper and deeper levels of our existence. It may begin with a delightful, intimate awareness of God as present in our room and become gradually a prayer of waiting. But in it all, it remains a dialogue between the two of us.

Prayer of the heart was for the writers of the devotional classics the basis for real prayer. Prayers said with our mouths had some value, for at least we praised Him with our mouths. A prayer life involving the mind, such as when we are actively working on our meditations, gets us below the surface into a still deeper relationship. But it is when we have begun to experience praying of the mind in the heart, listening and abiding prayer, that we know a deep conversation has begun. Our vocal prayers and meditations have prepared a receptive vessel in which the deeper dialogue could begin. Now God comes to us at deeper and deeper levels of prayer as we become sensitive instruments in all of our lives—a prayer without ceasing.

Thomas Merton said:

> The activity of the Spirit within us becomes more and more important as we progress in the life of interior prayer. It is true that our own efforts remain necessary, at least as long as they are not entirely superseded by the action of God 'in us and without us' (according to a traditional expression). But more and more our efforts attain a new orientation: instead of being directed toward ends we have chosen ourselves, instead of being measured by the profit and pleasure we judge they will produce, they are more and more directed to an obedient and co-operative submission to grace, which implies first of all an increasingly attentive and receptive attitude toward the hidden action of the Holy Spirit. It is precisely the function of meditation, in the sense in which we speak of it here, to bring us to this attitude of awareness and receptivity. It also gives us strength and hope along with a deep awareness of the value of interior silence in which the mystery of God's love is made clear to us.[1]

Prayer as conversation, as our response to God who is revealing Himself from moment to moment, is a way of living amid activity, a response of the heart which becomes then a way of resting in God. It becomes the language of the true self who finds life increasingly being integrated around the self-that-is-in-Christ. The life of prayer becomes a truly contemplative life. The call of all Christians is to be contemplatives, persons of prayer without ceasing; living lives in intimate, deep relationship with God; and out of it flowing streams of living waters.

The contemplative person is better able to live in the world without being squeezed into its mould of conformity. She is the person able to see the brokenness of society and move into it with a ministry and witness that are typified by caring and hope. The contemplative is able to enter into a loving dialogue with the world at deep levels of its infidelity to God's creative purposes, rather than denouncing and condemning the world. Prayer is an opening of our hearts at the deepest levels of our feelings and motivation to God in an expectant awareness that God is involved in and around us in each moment of the day, and we can respond to that activity.

Meditation Exercises

The meditation for this week will be built around an exercise to help you enter into dialogue with God through the events, persons, and experiences of each day. It will be a reflection on the activity of the previous day, a sort of digesting the events of the previous day, aimed at helping you become more aware *during* the day of your dialogue with the heavenly Father as those experiences are happening.

In your journal write down *each day* this week the following things about the previous day:

1. Reflect for a moment on yesterday. Try to recall all that went on during the day, the persons, activities, experiences. Just slowly let the entire day play back before your memory.

2. Now reduce the entire day to *one word*. What word best described the entire day?

3. What *object* that was part of yesterday's experience seems to express the day (for example, dishes, a typewriter, or a car)?

4. What *person* stands out during the day? If no one, write none.

5. What *joy* presented itself during the day (a good feeling, a thanksgiving, or a funny moment)?

6. What *difficulty* presented itself during the day? And what was the good or potential good that came of it?

7. Now reduce the entire day as a *gift* God gave to you. What was that gift?

As you do this *each day* for the next week, try to be conscious of living as freely as possible at *each moment* in the presence of God, at the cutting edge of each new moment, and in the fullness of life and reality of God.

5

'Wasting Time' for God

The pace of life in the Western world carries with it an illusion. We are so accustomed to having what we want and doing what we do 'as quickly as possible' that we do not realize what has been happening to us in the process. The illusion of saving time by being transported from one town to the next in aircraft has only pushed us into using that time to do more and more. What is saved in a dishwasher or clothes dryer is lost, in another activity. What has happened is that we find ourselves put out with anything and anyone who 'wastes time'. The adage that 'time is money' is one that has come into usage in the modern setting where we strive for efficiency, no lost motion, and above all speed.

The rush of our lives can cause us to suffer more strain, jangled nerves, high blood pressure, and heart illnesses. But physically, emotionally, relationally, and spiritually, we suffer even greater losses than we are aware. We need to learn how to 'waste time' again, so that time becomes a commodity to be used slowly, savouring each moment, allowing it to do its careful work within us and to us.

Wasting time for God is the third element in the inner work of God which allows us to live in a more transcendent awareness of life. It is basic to a deepening life of prayer and a life lived in abandonment to His presence. Wasting time for God simply means learning to love slowing down, silence and solitude. It means living life out of a deep transcendent integration, a 'quiet centre', from which words are spoken and life is lived at a deep enough level so that actions are made, not as reactions to another's action, but as responses to the inner promptings of our interior dialogue with self and God.[1]

How little of this silence, quietness, and inner solitude we really possess becomes apparent when we attempt to be quiet for just a few minutes. We become aware of the many distractions within and without. We feel an uneasiness and restlessness that causes us to seek relief in humming a tune, drumming our fingers on the table, or planning next week's schedule. When we introduce silence into a worship service, all kinds of coughing and shuffling of feet begin, and whispers and puzzled glances are exchanged asking, 'Who forgot what?'

Silence has not been praised in our society. Those who have begun to seek it somehow seem to have betrayed our cultural values of industriousness. Surrounded by technological systems that measure effectiveness of life by efficiency, the qualities of quietness, silence, and solitude are seen as negatives. We have been told too often, 'Idle hands are the devil's workshop', and so we don't feel comfortable with that much free space. And our inner turmoil is compounded by guilt in not producing anything in the silence. It seems to be the most unproductive of activities. Our uneasiness is felt when people ask us after a period of silent retreat, 'What did you do?' When our answer is, 'Nothing', their response is seen in their incredulity, if not downright hostility that we wasted that much time with nothing apparently to show for it.

What is missing for most of us is an appreciation of the rhythm that Jesus practised in his own life between activity and withdrawal. What we need to learn is how the two complement each other, and that one without the other leads to a sterility of life. There is both a sterility of non-reflective activity as well as one of escape from the world. Since most of us have to deal with the first more than the second, let's look at where we could be if we understood the necessary balance, according to our vocation in life, between activity and withdrawal; between working and waiting. We must also remember that whatever the balance of withdrawal and activity there is for us, there will be no meaningful deepening of the life of prayer nor of our abandonment to God unless we do have a time of withdrawal daily.

Reading through the accounts of the Gospel writers, one is struck with the fact that very often Jesus is in the midst of preaching, teaching, healing, or relating to a person, and the next minute He is withdrawing to pray. Now we have to understand that Jesus did not pray *just* when He withdrew. His entire life was one of dialogue with the Father, just as ours can be. But his withdrawal created free space out of which the living-in-depth-dialogue with the Father was possible during the rest of His daily activities. What we see here is that Jesus knew what it was to create within each day 'zones of silence' for more intense communication and meditation.

Jesus was able to slow down life in those moments, though others sought Him out, not understanding why He had taken Himself out of it for awhile (see the passages in Luke's Gospel that relate to this: 4.1 ff.; 4.42; 5.16; 6.12; 9.18, 28; 11.1; 21.37; 22.41 ff.). Even at one point of withdrawal, apparently seeing that this had so much meaning for Him, the disciples asked Jesus to teach them to pray.

Though prayer is not to be equated with withdrawal from activity, withdrawal is necessary for any serious life of prayer. Without silence, solitude, and quietness, any serious prayer life will be impossible. There must be a stilling of the mind, the heart, and the body in order for us to be able to listen. Those deeper dimensions of prayer are impossible if we are constantly flitting from one activity to another with no time in between for a simple resting in God.

So slowing down, solitude, and silence are withdrawals

from all the externals of life as we seek an interior freedom out of which life can be lived deeply within ourselves, with God, and in serious loving dialogue with the world. We are simply learning to practise the rhythm of Jesus. If we cannot disengage from life for brief moments each day, and for longer periods from time to time, life will be impoverished, and the true self as known by God will not be allowed to emerge.

Some have called this process 'centring down'. It has been described as a process by which we begin to still our outer lives in order to experience within us a quiet, calm centre out of which life can be lived. It has been called the silence which becomes the source of sound. Our first attempts at centring down may be clumsy and awkward. We make attempts at being quiet and still. We seek a place where we will not be disturbed—a room in the house, the still coolness of the sanctuary at the church, a rural retreat setting. And though we find that place and though the centre is there, we have been so accustomed to moving that it takes a long time to calm down. It is like a person suffering with inner ear problems. He continues to feel that his body is moving when it has really stopped, thus causing him to be disoriented and sick. It's like the flywheel of a great machine that has already had its motor stopped but continues to turn with the momentum left in it.

At first, centring down becomes a difficult task for us because we are so unaccustomed to it. The accumulation of the momentum of the day, weeks, months, and years carries us on with an inner restlessness that brings us to despair that we will ever be able to experience the deep, quiet waters within us. However, the more we work with it, the more we discover that a centring down can become possible quickly within any place, at any moment of the day. It becomes posssible to touch bottom and to know stillness and quietness in a crowded lunchroom, office, airport, bus ride, or amid thousands of people.

First, we must learn to be still, to turn off the external distractions of radio, television, newspapers, books, and hundreds of little things that demand time with us. We need to come to value silence and stillness as healing, friendly sound. Silence can be hostile, or it can be friendly space. It is hostile when we see it as wasted time. It is hostile when it seems to us as irrational, unproductive time.

Silence is above all hostile when we suddenly get in touch with the dimension of ourselves that lies just below the surface of our conscious awareness, and material from there begins to bubble to the surface, terrifying us as it emerges. We begin to encounter our hostility and anger. We experience our insecurities and helplessness. We begin to experience the falseness of ourselves. In the panic, we run back to hide under the constant sound of a radio, or an incessant conversation with someone, or the inane schedule of activities which blocks out that dimension of our lives which lies below the surface, only accessible to us in rare moments. We are accustomed to this escape in a life that values speed, swiftness, accomplishments, and efficiency. When too much activity begins to take its toll in our sleeping hours, we take a sleeping pill. Or if it affects us during our waking hours, we take a tranquillizer or other drugs. Avoidance of dealing with that material which lies below the surface of our conscious lives pushes us to attempt to live only at the conscious level, packing more and more into the unconscious until some day it explodes with an overload.

Silence, stillness, quietness, and solitude, though at times very painful as we experience our helplessness and nothingness, become the way towards more fruitful living. We need to study how to be quiet, to still the inner theatre of our lives, to find that quiet centre out of which God can be heard.

Elijah fled to the mountain of God where God had spoken to Moses in the thunder, lightning, and clouds, and didn't find God in the mighty wind, earthquake, or fire. It was in the low, gentle breeze (1 Kings 19.11 ff.). Silencing the externals leads to an inner silencing so that we may hear again. It may take us through the turbulence and momentum of our lives to that centre of stillness where we are able to hear once more.

It is an experience of being re-collected once more. Out of the fragmentation of ourselves, we learn the healing quality of stillness that allows the many fragments to be collected up again. We find ourselves once more sensing a wholeness of life.

The writers of the devotional classics have described the desert as the place of healing and wholeness. It was the place that offered no inherent attraction to mankind. It was desolate, still, silent, and foreboding. In it was no nourishment, and devils were said to inhabit the dry places. But the attraction of the desert to the followers of Christ in the early centuries was precisely because there in the desert they could come to experience an interior freedom that could not be found in a life of constant, undigested activity. They, like Moses, Elijah, Jesus, Paul, and many others, went there to learn the alternation between stillness and activity. And, when they were re-engaged in activity after the desert experience, it was an activity of a different quality and power. They had been able to gather the fragments of their lives into a new wholeness and to refocus life as those who knew the deep waters of recollection. Out of the deep well they had drawn the cool, clear, unpolluted waters of transcendent living.

Silence is friendly when it is felt to make possible that deeper communion with self, God, and the world around us. It is friendly as it begins to allow the boundaries of our existence to be stretched back, so we behold dimensions that we've never dreamed existed. It is friendly as we come to know the healing dimensions of being alone, still, and quiet. The fear of being alone is removed as we experience God at the deepest level of our being. It is friendly when we have not escaped the immediacy of God in the present moment. It is friendly as we come to experience in the solitude of the moment, the grounding of our past and future in Him who holds both. In solitude we can pay close attention to the world and ourselves and make an honest response to both.

In silence and solitude, we learn what constitutes too much activity in the rest of our existence and make a commitment to find just the right amount of activity which will allow us to live life deeply. In solitude, we learn to live in the world without being unduly shaped by it. In solitude, we learn to find an 'oasis of silence' within a busy schedule. In solitude, we learn to deal with our whole life in terms of what is enough and the freedom of not having to live under the tyranny of bigger and better, more and more.

First, we must learn to slow down life, embrace those times of silence, and experience the solitude of being alone with God. Each day should be marked off by a 'quiet time' where we can begin to learn the discipline of withdrawal and slowing down until that becomes a friendly, free space where we can come and go, where we can meet God for deeper moments of communion, and where the world can be seen in perspective. A daily quiet time at first is a discipline, but gradually we find it necessary if we are to live life deeply in the presence of God in each moment.

We begin by finding that place where we can be alone and undisturbed for the time we have set aside. We begin with a few minutes each day, increasing the time until we have found the amount of time that is needed for us to live with a sufficient depth in a transcendent awareness of ourselves, our relationships with others, and in an expectant awareness of God as He is revealing Himself in each moment.

For most of us, a daily quiet time begins with a period of silence in which we still the mind and the body so we can be totally present. It begins with an expectant awareness that God is present and that His word that day may hold the key to the rest of the day and our very existence.

Then we begin some process of a reflective nature which allows us to be more centred in God's purposes. It may be a gentle, meditative working with a part of the Scriptures (the Psalms, the Gospels, or one of the Epistles) in which we seek to get below the surface of the words and allow the dialogue of the pilgrimage of two thousand years ago to enter into dialogue with our daily pilgrimage. Or it may be a type of rhythmic praying with our breathing using the 'Jesus Prayer' (*Lord Jesus Christ/Son of God/Have Mercy on Me/a Sinner*) or part of one of the Psalms. It may be a meditative period on the created order of the universe. What we seek to do is to begin the dialogue with God through our own involvement in a gentle, meditative process of awareness of the God who has been active in history, and to bring our awareness of His activity into the *now* moment in which we are living.

As the period of quiet time deepens, our contemplative experiences expand and deepen. Not only do we deepen our awareness of ourselves, even the pain of our infidelities to the person Christ created us to be, but we also become more sensitive to God's Presence. We do not force Him to come to us, but just rest in the awareness that His movement in us is ever opening us outward and upward. We sense His guidance and His loving-kindness towards us. We sense His healing movements within us, and we begin to sense welling up within us the words of the psalmist,

> Bless the Lord, my soul;
>> my innermost heart, bless his holy name.
> Bless the Lord, my soul,
>> and forget none of his benefits.

He pardons all my guilt
and heals all my suffering.
He rescues me from the pit of death
and surrounds me with constant love,
with tender affection;
he contents me with all good in the prime of life,
and my youth is ever new like an eagle's.
Bless the Lord, my soul

(Ps. 103.1–5, 22, NEB)

A daily quiet time needs to be supplemented from time to time with longer periods of slowing life down, silence, and solitude. Retreats, in which one gets away from the daily routines of living and is engaged in another rhythm of activity, are necessary for longer and deeper moments of reflection, prayer, meditation, and contemplation. There need to be 'sabbaths of contemplation' during the busy schedules in which most of us live, in order to touch bottom at even deeper levels than we are able to maintain in our daily quiet times.

Even we find after a three-day retreat how little of the stillness and quietness we have yet been able to discover within ourselves. We discover the still flitting eddies of restlessness and distraction which hinder even deeper openness to ourselves and God. We learn that the silence in three days is both more hostile and more friendly than in thirty minutes or an hour a day. And, when we've come to know three days, we make an eight-day retreat, and find that it takes us three days just to get ready to begin drinking deeply of the waters that lie within and without us.

For too many, a retreat is not a disengagement and withdrawal from activity to be re-engaged at another level. It becomes simply another period of intense activity in which we are just as competitive, activistic, and tiring as the activities we left behind in order to come 'on retreat'. We play games, enjoy social fellowship, engage in all kinds of sports and recreation (and we have someone give us an 'inspiration-al' speech!), and we're off to another round of 'retreating'. This is not disengagement and withdrawal. It may be a good recreation weekend away, but it is not retreat.

Retreat is a time of learning to listen deeply in the silence and absence of activity. It is the communication with the stillness of life. It is listening deeply to self and to God. It is a time when longer periods of personal meditation and reflec-tion on the Scriptures become possible. It becomes a time to stand off from the whole process of civilized life and look at it, as if it were from a different altitude. A retreat, then, is conducted in complete silence, interrupted by sessions in which the retreat leader, through his brief presentations during the day, helps the retreatants explore other dimen-sions of their life in God. Then the retreatant returns to her own private work of listening, meditation, contemplation and writing in her journal, or reflective walks through the woods. Even the meals are conducted in silence, while one of the group reads from a book that adds additional insight to the theme of the retreat.

Places where individuals can go apart for several days alone are needed, where there is no programme but just the gentle allowing of a person to expand on that which is done in the daily quiet time. Instead of a brief time with a passage, a longer time can be given. Instead of a few moments of journalling, a longer time can be utilized, and even the journal can be reviewed for its deeper insights into one's life.

Whatever the type of retreat, it should move us to a deeper period of time that will result in a life lived even more deeply upon our return to whatever activity is ours. We need those places of silence, solitude, and rest. Too many religious camps, house parties and assemblies are geared to activity. They want to schedule every minute. Instead there need to be those places where a genuine resting in God can begin to take place as we learn that other dimension of our lives that is developed in 'wasting time for God'.

Ultimately, silence and solitude are to be found within, though we need those moments daily as well as occasional longer periods to allow us to touch the bottom of our deep, quiet centres. Inner solitude and the deep, quiet centre out of which life is lived should gradually become possible for us at any moment in the day, regardless of what the external surroundings are. It should be possible for us to learn enough of where that quiet centre is within us so that we may return to it many times during the day and live deeply out of it. We should gradually be able to live as centred and recollected persons amid the activity of life even as we do when we are engaged in our quiet time or retreat. But in order for inner solitude to take root within us, we must learn to be still, to love silence, and to be alone. There is a direct relationship between the periodic stilling of life and our capacity to live life deeply from an inner quiet centre.

Meditation Exercises

The meditation assignment for this week is Psalm 73.23–28. Follow the same process each day as described in chapter 1. A spiritual journey is a way of 'travelling through each day' more aware of God's activity in each expression of it. It is a way of being transcendently present to each person, event, circumstance as a moment of divine inbreaking.

Use a modern translation of the Psalm passage. Live with it all week. Memorize it, and let it become a prayer on your lips throughout the week. Work with it meditatively all week, pausing to allow each word to work its way into you and echo its claim on you.

Try to expand your quiet time this week by even five minutes or more if it's possible. Begin to find a place that will allow you to be alone and uninterrupted for your quiet time, not only while you are working on the exercises in this book, but also afterward when you seek to work on your own agenda.

This week practise slowing down life in every way possible. Instead of rushing to every activity, go at half the speed normally you would go. Allow yourself time to linger over your cup of coffee in the morning. As you walk around the office or in the house, walk slower than usual. Pause several times during the day to reflect on what has been happening around you. Go outside and look at the world around you and see things there you've never seen before. If you can, don't wear your watch this week. Without being irresponsible toward others, try to slow down your awareness about time. Try to 'waste some time with God' and not be aware of that time. Don't let the time on the watch determine how much time you should or should not spend with God. Sense the deep movement of your own heart and move in and out of the dialogue as you sense its movement within you.

Allow the entire week to slow down and seek to get in touch with your deep, quiet centre. Be aware of your restlessness and attempts to avoid dealing with silence and solitude. Record your feelings and attempts at silence in your journal, and become aware of the gradual slowing down of life, and of the inner dialogue with yourself and God which is taking place.

6

Seeing Things as They Really Are

One summer my family and I spent some time at one of the beaches of South Carolina. One evening as we were walking along the beach, we noticed people staring intently at the sand and walking very slowly. It was obvious that they were looking for something, but I wondered why there were so many doing it. It was easy to see that everyone was in on what was being looked for except us!

Finally, I stopped a lady and asked her what she was looking for, and she told me 'shark's teeth'. It seems that after high tide and the waves have brought new deposits of shells and sand to the beach, there is always a new deposit of the fossilized remains of those ancient monarchs of the seas. Actually we had been at the beach for several days, and though I had been walking on them, I hadn't seen a single shark's tooth! Yet, no more than two minutes after she told me what to look for, I saw one. As it turned out, it was one of the largest shark's teeth that we found as we worked at finding them the rest of the time we were there.

In the previous three chapters we have examined 'three tools' that God calls us to use in preparation for a more transcendent way of life: abandonment, prayer, and a daily quiet time. But we are not left alone in this ever deepening process of Christian growth. There are also three grace-gifts which enable our growth: discernment, disciplines, and community. We shall now look at the gift of discernment.

Jesus was concerned with whether his disciples could

really see. He often concluded a discourse, 'He who has eyes to see, let him see.' Or 'He who has ears to hear, let him hear.' Jesus was aware that just because we have two eyes and two ears, that did not guarantee either that we heard what was said or saw all that was going on around us.

Those who are on a pilgrimage with Christ are persons who are developing their capacity to see, what the New Testament refers to as the gift of discernment. Jesus said to those present who were candidates for being kingdom persons, 'Blessed are the pure in heart, for they shall see God' (Matt. 5.8, RSV). Søren Kierkegaard translated purity of heart as the capacity to will one thing.[1] Purity of heart is the singleness of vision that allows a person to see with a clarity that divided vision cannot. This was the concern of Jesus, that His disciples be able to see reality around them as it actually was.

Journeying more deeply into our deepest centre and into the world around us pushes us into seeing more deeply into all of life. Not only are we forced to deal with the illusions of our false selves but also the society around us. We find that much of what we thought was real is unreal and false. Much that we took for granted is thin and flimsy. Illusion is a thin vapour which, when pushed aside, reveals an entirely new way of viewing. In the Hirshhorn Museum in Washington, D.C., I saw a painting by Salvador Dali. At a distance it seemed like a skull staring at me with two empty sockets where there once were eyes. But at closer examination I saw that this was a painting of some monks at the burial of a friend. In the same building there was another painting by René Magritte entitled 'Delusions of Grandeur'. Using the famous pose of the Venus di Milo, it depicts a woman's body emerging out of itself at three different perspectives. Which is the real body? Using the cubist style for the sky, clouds seem to float across some cubes and not others. Which is the real sky? And a candle burns brightly in the midst of the daylight. Which is the real illumination? These artists, as many other modern painters, are dealing with what is real and what is simply illusion. The disciple of Christ, living closer and closer to God in a life that is open, available, abandoned, listening, and truly present, is one who begins to deal with the question of reality and illusion. Jesus begins to whisper, 'He who has eyes to see let him see!'

Seeing is difficult, especially when it is contrary to what we have been taught to see. We have a feeling that we are supposed to see things in a certain way, and when they do not present themselves to us in that way, we even have a tendency to bend facts to make them appear as they should be. That's one reason why racism is so difficult to eradicate, why peace and justice seem so elusive. We've been told that certain people are inferior, that war and poverty are inevitable, and we tend to see these issues in that light because we have become accustomed to seeing them that way.

Go into a grocery store. What do you see? We've been so conditioned to expect to see good, clean, wholesome food there that we hardly stop to ask, 'Is it?' How nourishing is the food there? How safe, clean, and pollutant free is it? Most of us have come a long way towards being able to tell which is nourishing food, which is junk food, which is empty calories and which is actually bad for our health. And, as more and more people become aware of this, the buying habits of many may begin to determine what food stores continue to carry.

What is necessary for seeing is to develop the eyes that can truly see all that is going on all around us. We need to see things 'from the other end', to see things 'as they really are', and to become what Glenn Hinson calls, 'horizontal Christians'[2] who can see things as they could be.

It is difficult, submerged in a particular society's values, to see things differently from that perspective we've grown up with. But that is exactly what Christ calls us to do. Jesus warned the disciples against the expectations of the religious leaders of their time: 'Beware of the leaven of the Pharisees' (Matt. 16.6, KJV). Their expectation was one of a Messiah who would be born in the system, who would aid in the upholding of the religious tradition, and would ultimately liberate the nation from foreign occupation. None of that was true of Jesus' life and ministry.

Jesus taught the disciples to see that persons were more valuable than sabbath laws; that persons' needs of food on the sabbath came before religious customs; that justice and mercy were desired by God more than sacrifices and temple observances. He helped them see that the woman, who was being tried for adultery, was of more value than legal satisfaction. He taught that ceremonial uncleanness was of lesser importance than helping a wounded traveller. Even Peter later discovered that keeping the dietary laws relating to meat was of lesser importance than sharing the way of salvation with a foreigner.

Jesus had to teach his disciples to see things from an entirely different direction. It was like making a 180 degree turn. It was seeing in one direction at one moment and then turning to see in just the opposite direction the next. The scriptural word is *metanoia*, or repentance. It means a turning around. To see is to turn all of the way around. It is to see that which is different from our accustomed perception.

It is as if one had grown up looking out on the outside world from a tunnel. All of your life, you had looked out at life through this one hollow tube that allowed you to see what was on the other side. You were able to see pretty well, and you grew accustomed to how things looked through that tube. Then one day you walked down that tunnel, and on the other side you turned and looked back. And the world that you now saw was entirely different. You were looking at things from the other end. That is what God is asking us to do. As we live into a life of availability, abandonment, and prayer, we begin to see things that we never saw before.

There is a reality to life in Christ that causes us to look deeply within and see the hollowness of much that we thought was real. As we look into the life of the church, much appears as chaff. We look out into the world and find a mess that we never dreamed was possible.

As we begin to see things from the perspective of God, we begin to see things from the other end. The values that we had placed on things begin to shift. The world around us begins to be seen with a reality that speaks of the deep wounds and fissures of society. We even begin to see the church with eyes that question its direction and its allegiance to Christ. We begin to see things from the point of view of eternity.

We cannot say that we see completely as God sees, but we begin slowly to gain the perspective of eternity. One of the things that begins to change within us is that, though there is a great deal of disturbance within us in seeing things as they really are, we also gain the viewpoint of God which is the capacity to see with patience, loving-kindness, and tender mercy.

As we gain the perspective of seeing from the other end, we also slowly begin to develop the capacity to 'see things as they really are'. William Stringfellow said that he believed that the greatest gift for any generation, and especially ours—outside of faith, hope, and love, which are the enduring gifts of God—was the gift of discernment; the capacity to see things in perspective.[3] The one who begins to live deeply as a contemplative, begins to see things are they really are. The illusions and the real become very apparent in self and the world. Persons who are willing to pay the price of being inward people soon begin to see things as they really are. They become 'contemplative critics', and how few of them there are.

Thomas Merton asked.

> I wonder if there are twenty men alive in the world now who see things as they really are. That would mean that there were twenty men who were free, who were not dominated or even influenced by any attachment to any created thing or to their own selves or to any gift of God, even to the highest, the most supernaturally pure of His graces.[4]

Merton answered his own question by saying he did not believe that there were that many who could see reality that clearly, but felt that there must be at least one or two, and 'they are the ones who are holding everything together and keeping the universe from falling apart'.[5]

Why are we blind then? Why don't we see things as they really are? Who are the one or two in your church, denomination, city, nation or world who see things as they really are? How is it that they can see and we can't? Or do we just simply write them off as 'being out of step with the rest of us'?

Certainly there is within each of us something which avoids reality. We merely resist seeing. We have certain categories through which we filter everything. If the new information fits, then we accept it. Otherwise, we reject it, we rationalize it away, ignore it, or repress it. Arthur Combs has said that our resistance to seeing is in direct relationship to how threatening the new information is to our perception of ourselves.[6] Those concepts of ourselves which form the core of our personality either enhance the understanding of who we are, or threaten that understanding.

This is the crucial point for a follower of Christ who is attempting to deal with his real self, the self that is becoming, and the false self which must die. The follower of Christ is just as threatened as anyone, and maybe more so, as he attempts to deal with the reality around him as seen from

God's perspective. The falsity that he finds in the core of his being attempts to flee from Christ's penetrating gaze.

The words of the guides in spiritual growth of previous centuries have always indicated that spiritual growth is not the achievement of utopia or nirvana. That is not to say that spiritual growth is masochistic or that spiritual growth seeks the destruction of the self. What they have indicated is that spiritual growth is a never-ending process of constant awareness of our infidelity to our own inner truth as self-in-Christ and a continual quest of being that true self.

This is a road of much anguish, tears, and inner suffering. And many are the times when we wonder why we ever took this road in the first place. Then we remember that Christ's call to discipleship is a call to deal with our inner journey as we also journey into witness and ministry. Otherwise, as we share in our outward journey, if we have not dealt sufficiently with our own interior landscape, we give out of the 'contagion of our own sickness', rather than the promise, hope, and love of the 'good news'.

Thus for the one following Christ, seeing things as they really are, from the other end, begins with oneself. Though that means working against the inner organization of all our previous perceptions, we must begin with a reorganization of all that we see in light of the revealed Word of God and His inner light of grace. As painful as that is to us, it is necessary to experience a destabilizing work in our lives in order to be restabilized around the Christ-centre in our deepest self. That means an opening within us to be able to see, even if seeing the light of God hurts our eyes as it strikes deeply into our infidelity.

Many of the self-concepts which hinder us from seeing reality may be so rooted in the core of our being that a lifetime will hardly be sufficient for them to be completely rooted out. But in our calling to follow Christ, we are called to see even if the pain of seeing hurts deeply. Peter said to Jesus, after he realized that Jesus was the Lord of the sea and that the haul of fish was larger than he could have ever imagined after a night of unsuccessful fishing, 'Depart from me, for I am a sinful man, O Lord' (Luke 5.8, RSV). The penetrating light of the Master's truth burned into his own inner unfaithfulness, and it hurt. According to Luke, this is the calling of Peter to be His disciple. That call is both a healing light as well as the illumination of our infidelity. Peter, as we will find in our own lives, had to continue to encounter the infidelity of his inner core which did not allow him to see the necessity of Jesus' death, his own denial of the Lord, the call to witness to the Gentile centurion, and even his own way of dying.

That which hinders us most from seeing things as they really are lies within us. We do not see the obvious around us because of preconceived ways of seeing. We have a selective seeing which sees what confirms the falsity within us and ignores that which does not confirm our true being. But ours is a calling to sort out the real from the unreal. We are not to assume that all which appears to us as real is actually real. Ours is a call to be those who, out of our inward walk with God, see at a level below the surface of things and distinguish between reality and appearances.

Seeing does not mean that we insist that only the supernatural is real, and the natural is evil and therefore unreal. Those who seek to follow Christ must become what Henri Nouwen said of Thomas Merton, 'contemplative critics'.[7] We are to be those who are called to live life in the world and to plumb the depths of situations and events in the light of our contemplative experiences with God. We are called to see, not in our own subjective isolation, but to enter into a contemplative dialogue with the world.

We are not angry denouncers of the world, as if God did not love the world and had not sent His son to die for it. We are to be those who continue to deal with the illusions of ourselves and slowly begin to see God's purposes in the unfolding of things, so we can enter into a loving dialogue with the world. Because of contemplative silence, we begin to see the activity of the Father in ways we have never seen before. Our contemplation does not allow us to be turned away from the world, as if fleeing from the world and persons were our goal. We are called to embrace the world, but with eyes that have begun to practise the gift of discernment. We do not turn our backs on the world in contempt as we journey deeper and deeper into ourselves and God. Instead, we turn with a singleness of vision that is able to see God in each new situation, every person, and experience, and see those things in a truer perspective.

Having begun the task of unmasking illusion in ourselves, we begin to discern with eyes of faith the inner significance of the events, experiences, and situations around us. This means that we are bound to search out the reality of things as they really are. We begin to deal with the economic realities, the social and political realities, the governmental and business realities, the realities of relationships and understandings. All of life now stands under our gaze, and by inner dialogue with the Father we are led into a deepening relationship with the world around us.

Now the quest for the capacity to see leads us to 'seeing things as they can be'. Inevitably, as we begin to focus on things as they are, we can become depressed at the difficult tangle of things in the world. A sort of hopelessness and despair begins to set in on us. We want to throw up our hands and say it is impossible. But faith, hope, and love are the Father's gifts to His world through us. We are the ones who have been given access to a vision that world powers despise and reject. We are those who have not only been given the gift of seeing, discernment, but we have also been given access to the power to bring hope to chaos, faith to insoluble problems, and love to face the power of demonic systems.

With this we can better see our calling to be 'horizontal Christians'. As such, we are able to look over the horizon and see what could be. This is not a seeing of ought and duty. It is a seeing of could's and possibility. It is a seeing of what could happen by persons who have looked within and without and are not discouraged by the seemingly impossible. We are those who ask the question, 'Why not?'

Why does war and poverty have to be? Why do the oppressed have to remain unfree? Why can't liberation be for all oppressed people? Why are black, brown, and yellow peoples of the earth not considered people of worth by some?

Why do the few consume the most? Can there not be an equal access to the basic needs for all people? Why do world affairs have to be controlled by multi-national business interests, rather than by the people? Why do people have to be exploited in the name of profit? Why do people have to be hungry? Is there not enough food for all? Why do some people diet while others starve?

Why do we warehouse our sick, old, young, retarded, mentally ill, delinquent and dying—our unwanted people? Why do we say we are for peace and yet increase our instruments of war? Why do our cities have to decay? Why do we always have to have a bigger profit margin than the year before, while we die from the air we breathe, the pesticides we ingest, and the empty calories we substitute for nourishment?

As horizontal Christians, we have the capacity to see things as they could be and ask, 'Why not?' I believe that there are some who are seeing things as they can be and are willing to pay the price to see this happen. Many people never make the headlines in our newspapers though they are travelling for peace in the world, making housing available to the poor, working on food systems for the hungry, championing the rights of the oppressed, stopping the pollution of streams and the air, and giving hope and care to the forgotten. They continue their work because, in seeing things as they really are, they have also asked, Why not?

Meditation Exercises

This week seek to become more aware of what God is doing all around you. Develop eyes that can see deeply. Try to see things, not from your end of the tunnel, but from the other end. Ask those questions of what you find, both in yourself and what you see in the world around you, that will seek to discern what is real and what is illusion.

To help you become more aware of this, at the beginning of each day this week, use an exercise called the 'plotted day'. At the beginning of each day, look at the activities that that day will bring, the ones that you know you will be involved in during the day. Looking over the list of activities, ask God's guidance as you are involved in that activity or meeting with that person or group of persons. Ask Him to make you aware of His presence, so you can see all that is going on.

I know a nurse who uses this practice at the beginning of her round of duties with hospital patients. She begins each day with a prayer for each person as she goes down the list of persons assigned to her and asks God to make her aware of that person's needs, so she can truly be a minister to that person that day. I know a businessman who looks at his calendar of activities at the beginning of each day and asks God to help him be aware in every way of what God is doing in and through him with those persons he meets that day.

Use the plotted day, even if yours is a schedule that is not as structured as these two. Just ask God to help you see this day in a way you have never seen before; to be aware of persons, things, events, and experiences at a deep level of meaning.

Use a newspaper and glance at the headlines—don't read it in detail—and try to get below the surface of what is happening in the world where you live.

Finally, be aware of the interruptions and unplanned events and persons God sends you during the day. Try to see each one of them as an opportunity for growth and ministry. See in each one of them God's activity of a 'sculptor modelling his clay'. It just could be that if you are attentive, you may be able to discover God's activity around you, the ministry needs of people and situations, and nudge yourself into new and more demanding dimensions of your own Christian maturity.

Record in your journal each day what happened as you sought to become more aware that day of the events, the experiences, the people that *this* day brought to you. What did you see for the first time? What message is there in it for you?

For your Scripture meditations, this week work with Psalm 104.

7

Like a Glass Emptied of Water

As we journey deeper and deeper into life with God, we find that there also must be a corresponding narrowing of the exterior life. This is the second gift of God in knowing an interior freedom that allows us to follow Christ more deeply, His gift to us of spiritual disciplines.[1] When we come to love the inner work of God, we come to know the necessity of constriction of the outward life as well. As it is necessary to still the body and mind to be present completely to the Lord, so there is a corresponding necessity to bring under control appetites, drives, habits, tastes, and trappings of our inauthentic life-style, so that we may learn a freedom that detaches us from things that control us, even unconsciously. It is a dying at one level in order to become alive at another.

The writer of Hebrews said of Jesus: 'Son though he was, he learned obedience in the school of suffering, and, once perfected, became the source of eternal salvation for all who obey him' (Heb. 5.9-9, NEB). And Paul said:

> For the divine nature was his from the first; yet he did not think to snatch at equality with God, but made himself nothing, assuming the nature of a slave. Bearing the human likeness, revealed in human shape, he humbled himself, and in obedience accepted even death—death on a cross. Therefore God raised him to the heights and bestowed on him the name above all names, that at the name of Jesus every knee shall bow—in heaven, on earth,

78

and in the depths—and every tongue confess, 'Jesus
Christ is Lord', to the glory of God the Father (Phil.
2.6–11, NEB).

Paul, as did Jesus, knew the costliness of interior freedom.
To the Philippians he said:

> I have learned to be satisfied with what I have. I know
> what it is to be in need, and what it is to have more than
> enough. I have learned this secret, so that anywhere, at
> any time, I am content, whether I am full or hungry,
> whether I have too much or too little. I have the strength to
> face all conditions by the power that Christ gives me (Phil.
> 4.11–13, GNB).

To the church at Corinth, he said:

> We recommend ourselves by the innocence of our be-
> haviour, our grasp of truth, our patience and kindliness;
> by gifts of the Holy Spirit, by sincere love, by declaring
> the truth, by the power of God. We wield the weapons of
> righteousness in right hand and left. Honour and dishon-
> our, praise and blame, are alike our lot: we are the
> impostors who speak the truth, the unknown men whom
> all men know; dying we still live on; disciplined by
> suffering, we are not done to death; in our sorrows we have
> always cause for joy; poor ourselves, we bring wealth to
> many; penniless, we own the world (2 Cor. 6.6–10, NEB).

Both Jesus and Paul learned an interior freedom through
the school of obedience and discipline. Discipline, which is
so distasteful to us, is really the school for followers of Christ.
Both *disciple* and *discipline* come from a common root and
have to do with learning. A disciple is one whose learning is
discipline (the teaching, or learning, of a follower). Equating
discipline with punishment has come only as whippings and
beatings were used to gain outward conformity. The real

arena of discipline is an inner one. Outward conduct conforms to inner realities.

We are attached to many things that keep us from being free. Some of these are conscious attachments; many others are unconscious attachments. The costly work of becoming a learner of Christ goes on within us. The more we seek to be free, detached, abandoned, and available, the more we realize that we are not free; that the attachments of our lives have their roots deep within us. As much as we seek to maintain a life of constant awareness of God's activity in and around us, the more we are in touch with the many distractions that call us to look here, go there, do this. We begin to learn that we are dealing with an illusory reality within ourselves.

Jesus told His disciples, in essence, 'The things that you love will tell you where you are' (compare Luke 6.45; 12.34). Therefore, it was necessary for them, as it is for us, to root out the attachments in order to be those who are free enough to be able to hear God's slightest whisper. As we begin to get in touch with these attachments, even the secret ones of which we may only be faintly aware, we find out that our judgements, choices and decisions are heavily influenced by these attachments which do not leave us indifferent to God's good pleasure for us and His world.

Our motives are seen for what they are. They are nothing more than the rationalizations about the infidelity which God calls to our attention. They are the smokescreens behind which we hide and practise our outward pieties.

Jesus spoke to His disciples about the problem of divided loyalties which caused them to be easily distracted from following Him. In the parable of the soils (Matt. 13.22–23), He said that such preoccupations 'choke the word of God and render the person unfruitful.' He warned his disciples against trying to serve 'God and money' (Matt. 6.24, GNB). To the young man who wanted to take care of his religious obligations before following Christ, Jesus replied, 'Anyone who starts to plough and then keeps looking back is of no use to the Kingdom of God' (Luke 9.62, GNB).

The divided kingdom within us is the terrain of discipline. It is there that we begin to encounter our resistances to discipleship. The desire to go with Christ, wherever He calls us, is countered by the division within. Distractions to other things easily carry us off from the work of the kingdom. Soon, we find that our ability to follow Christ as agilely and responsively as we once did is gone, and we have forgotten what He said for us to do.

Only as we submit ourselves to the School of Christ do we learn what He learned, obedience and humility. Though He was the Son of God, He did not fall back on that to keep Him from learning obedience, which made Him more available to the accomplishment of His mission of being the means of salvation for others. Only as we learn in the School of Discipline will we become more completely available to God's will in our lives.

Discipline to the Christian is what form or a medium is to the artist. Every artist must allow her creativity and spontaneity to flow through the limiting, restricting confines of the media she is working with. For the artist it is attempting to convey the inner image she sees by means of the medium of oils and canvas, a piece of marble, or the lens of a camera. There are limitations, even using them, to express what she sees. The writer has to do the same with words. And the Christian allows the focusing of life to be channelled through the disciplines that he accepts and finds given to him in order to be shaped by the creative work of God.

Just as the medium the artist uses shapes her art, so do the disciplines shape the followers of Christ. They say who we are. They describe our understanding of the life-style we have found in Christ. And they also shape us in the direction in which we would like to be going. The banks of a river serve this purpose to guide and channel the energies of the river. So do the disciplines guide and channel the follower of Christ as he proceeds along the journey.

A personal discipline might be:

— a daily encounter with God in Scripture study and prayer;

— participation in a study group in order to be an informed, mature Christian;

— engagement out of one's gifts in some continuous expression of ministry and witness to the brokenness of the world;

— giving sacrificially, beginning with the tithe;

— worshipping weekly with the group of people with whom you form part of the Body of Christ.[2]

This might be considered a basic discipline for a new Christian, but the costliness of even this much becomes readily apparent as one begins to work with it. A daily quiet time begins to weigh heavily upon us, and its constraints begin to confine us as we get involved in other activities. First thing we know, we begin to excuse ourselves from it, saying, 'I will have my quiet time today as I wash the dishes, or drive to work.' Then what happens is that we no longer exist within the tension of a life lived deeply in the Scriptures and in dialogue with God.

No longer can we be described as persons of the Book, or a people of prayer. We have become a people of busyness. Thus, we can see how the discipline begins to describe us and shape us. When we cease to do it, we are defined and shaped by whatever takes its place.

The same is true of study, ministry, witness, or stewardship of money, and our corporate worship. If these are not the disciplines that describe and shape us as the people of God, what then is taking their place? Is it bowling, eating, clothes, television, recreation, work, duty, walking away from need, golf, fishing, a larger house, bigger car, the best furniture—what?

To these, some would add other disciplines which are shaping their lives in Christ, such as: occupational accountability which avoids the creation of products which cause harm to others; commitment to a life of economic simplicity so as to be able to share their personal wealth with the world's hungry and poor; commitment to reshaping institutions in order to bring about a more just global society in which each person has full access to the needed resources for their physical, emotional, intellectual and spiritual growth; commitment to an ecologically sound world free from pollutants in the air, waterways, oceans, and land; commitment to the cause of peace and non-involvement in war; and commitment to the elimination of racism, injustice, hunger, poverty, inadequate housing and illiteracy.

Each of these, consciously accepted, becomes a way of disciplining life. And the greatest discipline is the discipline of freedom from the self-sufficient, go-it-alone self within us. This is where God and we must work out the interior freedom of our lives. Working at this level prevents us from being satisfied with silly little sacrifices in the name of discipline. 'I give up this, or I give up that,' just will not begin to make a dent in the interior freedom that needs to be ours. Those who have tried to impose do's and don't's on people not only have settled with an exterior conformity, but have missed the point of contending with that which keeps us from being free, as well as that which describes us as persons-in-Christ.

There is little or no deep spiritual growth without disciplines which describe and shape us in our Christian walk. As we work with our attachments and seek to become free of them, we also have to experience that shaping from within that disciplines effect. Though the outward conformity is not enough, we need to have that guiding and channelling of doing certain things until inner controls begin to take over. This was the hope of those who advocated 'don't spare the rod'. Though much of what happened during that era was inhuman, there was a certain truth in those who also said, 'as a twig is bent, so grows the tree.' However, too many depended on bending the twig and hoping that would do it. As many who have struggled with inner disciplines can verify, that is not sufficient guarantee that inner controls have been developed.

Disciplines ultimately have to work with our inner dimensions. Many of those who have written of the spiritual life have pointed to the need to work even more deeply within ourselves than just the prescribing of rules of conduct. This work is designated by the term *asceticism*. Unfortunately, asceticism has come to mean an austerity and a rigorous abstention which scares us. For many, asceticism suggests images of sadistic self-abuse.

As is true with the image of discipline, asceticism has been wrongly discarded because of its abuses. The true ascetic is a person who has learned that fasting, austerity, long periods of prayer, self-control, and denial of certain things (which may be good within themselves) has a way of opening up within us new dimensions of freedom, which otherwise stay closed when life is lived mainly at the level of gratifying every urge we have.

Jesus taught the disciples about fasting. He never questioned whether His followers should fast. He just instructed them about it. First, He told His disciples not to practise fasting as an outward show, as the Pharisees did (Matt. 6.16–18). Fasting was to be accompanied by an interior dialogue with the Father, so the exterior of the person was to be groomed, washed, and joyful. If fasting were only an exterior matter, then the Pharisees were right in changing their appearances, having long faces.

Second, said George Maloney,[3] Jesus taught the disciples that fasting has an eschatological significance (Matt. 9.15). In a real way, a person gets in touch with the deeper meaning of the presence and absence of the Lord. The disciples did not fast when Jesus was present, but fasted after His departure which became 'part of that eschatological waiting in sorrow and suffering until the Bridegroom comes in all His splendour and glory'.

As pilgrims on a journey, periods of fasting allow us to dialogue with the meaning of Jesus' death, burial, and resurrection as we await His return. It is a way for us to enter into the deeper understandings of our own participation in ministry with Him until He comes again. Jesus began His own ministry through a forty-day fast. 'A result of His fasting was to receive illumination on the Father's will and to reach that degree of conformity to the Father to do His will at whatever cost.'[4] He affirmed this when he said, 'Man cannot live on bread alone, but needs every word that God speaks' (Matt. 4.4, GNB). Prayer and fasting are linked by Jesus as inseparable ways of dialogue with the Father.

Discipline leads us to a greater dependence on God in obedience and humility. Ultimately, the goal is to teach us an indifference to God's will for us. As Paul said in the letter to the church at Corinth (2 Cor. 6.6–10), he went through all kinds of difficulties, yet with a spirit of indifference to whatever was his state. He had come to know that God was working out in each and every circumstance the good that He willed. As Paul said later, 'Moreover we know that to those who love God, who are called according to his plan, everything that happens fits into a pattern for good' (Rom. 8.28, Phillips).

As we come to experience our own poverty in fasting, a new consciousness develops within us that allows us to see

God's purposes with clarity. We understand a little better what is enough in this consumer-oriented society of bigger and better, more and more. We begin to understand that our trust is not entirely in God, and we learn the painful detachment that must take place in obedience and humility to Him. We begin to get in touch with the simplicity of life itself which brings a freeing and refocusing of time, money and effort. As Thomas Merton said,

> It means detachment and freedom with regard to inordinate cares so that we are able to use the good things of life and able to do without them for the sake of higher ends. It means the ability to use or sacrifice all created things in the interest of love.[5]

Discipline is the call to interior freedom in which God asks us to empty our vessels, so that He may fill them with His gifts. As Jesus did at Cana, we are like a glass emptied of water to be filled with exquisite wine.

Meditation Exercises

The Scripture to be worked with this week is John 15.1–17. Follow the same process each day as described in chapter 1.

Begin to work out the disciplines that describe you. Where would you like to be in your spiritual life five years from now, and what disciplines will help you get there? For example, if you should say that you would like to have a richer prayer life, how much time will you begin to spend now in your quiet time which will allow you to live at that depth then?

Look back over your journal entries for the past six weeks and see if you discover any attachments that might indicate places where you could begin to work on your own interior freedom. What other issues are you aware of which do not allow you to be free to hear and obey God's call to you?

Where do you find divided loyalties within you? How have

these worked against your true self? Since disciplines are but
the scaffolding which is used to construct the building and
are useless once the building is in place, what are these
disciplines pointing you towards?

Again record these in your journal.

8

The Gift of Community

The third element in interior freedom is found in the gift of
community. On the surface it may seem strange that our own
inner freedom is found in the charisma of community.
However, we begin to see its relationship very quickly as we
understand that the inner work of God in us is never com-
pleted unless we have each other.

A church is not basically a big business. It is not primarily a
promotional organization. It does not exist to think up
programmes to keep people busy. Its function is not to
measure itself constantly as a patient with a thermometer in
his mouth. It was not created to succumb to the hucksterism
of the marketplace. It is not to be equated with buildings and
facilities. It is more than programmes, budgets, and number
of staff. Its address is not fixed at 1311 Main Street. It has
more assets than are listed on the annual financial statement.
It is not the local outlet for the national programme. It is
basically *community*.

Community is that place where we enter into the presence
of each other and the Lord who called us there, as fully and
totally as we do in the engagements with ourselves and God.
It is a place that calls us to abandon ourselves to each other,
for in so doing, we discover ourselves. It is a place where we
are available to each other as we have learned to be with God.
It is a place where we are totally present to each other, aware
of each other, and are listening to each other with the totality
of our being. It is a coming together because Christ has called
us to be committed to Him and to each other through His gift
of *koinonia*.

Community is our new family, not based on chromosomes or proximity. We are there because God called us there and because we choose to respond to His call. Communities based on blood-ties and togetherness are strained when the call of Christ to discipleship is obeyed, said Jesus (Matt. 12.46–50; 10.21–23, 34–39). But a new family is given to compensate for that which was pulled apart in obedience to Him (Matt. 19.29), one based on God's gift. Thus community is gift. You are gift to me, and I am gift to you. God has given us each other for the working out of our salvation. I am not community to you by accident, nor you to me. We have been given to each other for a purpose. The longer I stay with you and you with me, the more we will discover that purpose.

Therefore our commitment to each other in community can never be a tentative one. We are not with each other in community as long as 'We are getting something out of it', or 'Until we can find a better place to go,' or 'As long as we get along with each other'. We are not in community with each other just to attend services together. We can do that in many places. We are here because we have been given to each other by God to allow us to become our true selves.

There are times when I wonder why God gave me this particular group of 'miserable, faltering sinners' to have to live with. If I had done the choosing, I would have chosen a better group of people to live my life out with. You are not like me. True, there are one or two with whom I have something in common, but with many of you—in fact, too many—I have nothing in common. We don't think alike on issues. We don't dress alike. Our occupations take us to different places, and we are around different people during the day. I don't understand why God has given me such an unlikely group of people as you—but He has. Sometimes I wish He had given me a group of people who could really understand me, be more compassionate toward me, and love me a little more. But He knew I needed you, and I am beginning to see why I need you.

Community is not made up of the same kind of people. If God were to organize churches the same way we organize social clubs, political organizations, unions, or professional societies, we would not have that person whom we need to help us be complete. God did not organize the church on the basis of sameness. True, there is the element of *unity* emphasized within the church, but sameness is never valued as the foundation of the church. In fact, James specifically admonished the church against it (Jas. 2.1 ff).

Unity in any community is found in the words of Paul to the church at Ephesus: 'Do your best to preserve the unity which the Spirit gives, by the peace that binds you together. There is one body and one Spirit, just as there is one hope to which God has called you. There is one Lord, one faith, one baptism; there is one God and Father of all men, who is Lord of all, works through all, and is in all' (Eph. 4.3–6, GNB). That is the unity of a common Lord and a common call—a unity which is a gift of the Spirit.

I am in community with you because God has called both of us to discipleship in Christ. The same Spirit who called you has also whispered in my heart the same message, 'Jesus is Lord!' Because neither of us could have said that on our own, we know that it is the same Spirit who enabled us to make that confession of faith. And He is the One who has made us brother and sister to each other in a way no earthly birth could have done.

Jesus is Lord! That is our common birth, and our common call to community. We stay in community because it has been provided to us as gift-for-our-growth. There are depths of ourselves we will never experience and know unless we live our lives in community. We have the capacities for living with our illusory self and thinking it is real. Only as we are allowed to live into a relationship with each other, can we come to know the real self, both the gifted side of ourselves as well as the darker side that we do not know, but the other person can see clearly.

You can help me know both dimensions of myself. Yours is a gift of acceptance and affirmation of me. I sense your loving-kindness towards me, and this helps me know even more deeply the Father's loving-kindness for me. You accept me, 'warts and all', just as I am. I know that you probably wish, as I, that you had a better specimen to work with, but your willingness to allow me to walk with you, even though I am wounded, bleeding, hostile, angry, and not knowing why I'm that way, has created a free space for me to be me.

I've learned to relax the barriers within me when I am around you because you will not reject me, even when the 'darker self' begins to act out of self-hatred. Where there was ambivalence towards you and anyone else I did not know—and therefore tried to predict how you would accept or reject me—I now begin to experience the beginnings of spontaneity. I am able to react as I really feel. I am able to tell you what I am thinking because I know you will not reject me.

I don't mean that you haven't disagreed with me. You have, and yet when we greet each other the next time, there still is peace between us. With others I know what would have happened is they wouldn't have spoken for days. They would have pouted and tried to cut me down from behind their defences. But you allowed me to lower mine the day you risked being vulnerable. You showed me the wounded side of you, the side that hasn't got it all together. I was shocked at first because you had seemed to me to be 'Mister Cool'. But I came to know you as human like me, for what you said was what I had been experiencing—I knew it deep down inside of me—but I couldn't admit it to anyone, least of all myself.

We shared our inadequate feelings, but you were quick to

begin sharing what good you saw in me. It was hard to listen to you talk about my good qualities, for I knew too well where I was weak, selfish, clumsy, and ignorant. But you continued, and you helped me through your affirmations to know that there was a side of me that is beautiful. I think the greatest sin I know of is the withholding of affirmation from another. You have taught me this. And now I know that there are others besides you whom God has given me to practise this ministry of affirmation. I know how it is to have existed so long in my life never thinking of myself as worthy or worth anything at all and how your affirmation of me changed that. Now, the gift of affirmation is mine to give another.

Community is a place of acceptance and affirmation. It is a way of being together, but at a much deeper level than just being physically together in a room or at a church function. It is a way of sensing a common unity that binds each person together in a way that becomes gift. But community is not just peaches and cream. Just as there is a dark side of each of us as well as a gifted side, so there is a dark side of community.

The hunger to be part of a caring, sharing, loving, affirming community in recent years has blocked off our sight of the dark side of community. Communities, if they are genuine and not just superficial togetherness which seeks to keep tranquillity at all costs, are places of facing and dealing with suffering, estrangement and loneliness. Every genuine community has to deal with its dark side as well as its gift-giving side; its growing edge as well as its gains and victories. For this reason, we can't just live in community during the bright, sunshiny day and abandon it when it has to go through one of its periodic times of tension, suffering, and re-integration.

As a pilgrim people, a community is constantly dealing with the level of trust; how much can we risk together; its times of instability; the not-yets; the rough edges; and its incompletenesses. These are time when we wonder why we are in community at all. We question deeply what we are doing there. There's just too much pain and suffering in our world to have to go through it also in community. We've come there for healing, loving, caring, trust, and hope. What we find is brokenness, mistrust, fear, anxiety, loneliness, and despair. Sometimes it's just too much. We don't know whether we can endure any more.

At those times, we feel deep within us anger and a desire to shake the other one until his teeth rattle, trying to get him to regain his senses again. But then we realize the anxiety is within us. If we were more at home within ourselves, we would allow other persons the free space to be themselves, even in our anger.

Then there are times when I would commit myself to you, but I don't know if you are worthy of my costly commitment. You seem to be so fragile, wounded, and incapable of doing any good. I don't know whether my trust will be returned; so I wait on you to make the first move of commitment, to indicate that you are worthy of risking my life with you. Then I remember that Jesus didn't have a person who was worthy in the whole group of twelve. The commitment that I am asked to make is not just to you but to Christ, and so I take the first step. I risk it, even if neither you nor anyone else goes with me, because that's my call, and I must be obedient to it.

There's a cost in community, as well as a promise. The cost is the tension that comes with living with a group of 'miserable, faltering sinners' and allowing something of each one of us to be given up in order to know the corporate dimensions of love, hope, and a deep abiding faith. In this age of individualism, of seeking after our own spontaneity, there is also the ingredient of interdependence, of unity within diversity. We talk a good deal about these ideals, but very few persons experience the depths of living in community where we are accountable to each other.

There is a need for creativity and spontaneity in persons. Too many of us today have lost the innocence of spontaneous behaviour. We are so controlled and guarded in our behaviour that we walk around as tiny robots all wound up, with only one direction to go—the direction we've been programmed to go in. But as we begin to experience creativity at deeper dimensions of our lives, there is another ingredient, a group of people with whom we can live out the costliness of discipleship. Extreme individuality results in anarchy while extreme corporateness results in a loss of personhood. But spontaneity within community allows for a depth of growth that is not possible in either extreme individuality or corporateness.

In community we are encouraged to take the risk of creativity because of the loving, caring persons around us. They call forth our gifts and hold us accountable in the exercising of them. They speak to us at the deep dimensions of our lives. They do not allow us to live superficially in the shallows of the deep waters that lie within us. They urge us to drink deeper and deeper. And they also make us aware of our resistances, wounds, and blockages to growth. They help us know when we are leading out of wound rather than creativity. They put us in touch with the shallowness with which we content ourselves in the area of creativity. They remind us that there are still untapped sources within, and they urge us on.

When we begin to resort to old tactics and strategies for coping with life, they make us aware of our regressions. They help us restore patterns of living that have not become ingrained enough to have become a pattern for living. When anger and hostility rise up within us, they allow space, but also point out the inadequacies of our behaviour without destroying us. They show their displeasure with our actions, but never reject us.

Accountability is different from a passive submission to, or trying to re-create 'over-under' obedience structures with new names. Jesus said to his disciples, 'No longer do I call you *doulos* (slave) because a *doulos* does not know his master's business; I call you *philous* (friends) because everything I have learned from my Father I have made known to you' (John 15.15). We are no longer slaves but friends. This is no chain-of-command structure, nor one of grovelling subservience to one in authority. This is an accountability of love. Jesus had told His disciples to beware of the Pharisees' way of exercising authority. They 'placed heavy burdens on men's shoulders', 'liked to be seen', took the 'chief places' in church, liked to have men 'greet them', and wanted to be called 'our teacher' [rabbi] (Matt. 23.1–7).

Instead, Jesus said that you are *not* to call one of you 'our teacher', for I am your Teacher, and you are brothers to each other; nor are you to designate one of yourselves as 'father', for God is your Father; neither are you to call yourselves 'leader', for I am your only Leader; and the *greatest* one among you is a *diakonos* [servant] (Matt. 23.8–12).

Accountability in community is a corporate holding of the cost/promise tension active in each of us, so our brokenness can be healed and life can be lived out of our gifts. No system of ten laws, five roads, or a chain of command slavishly obeyed, can offer that growth. Growth produces tension and is itself nurtured by the tension. God's ministry of 'holy discomfort' ministers to us over and over again as He constantly asks us to leave the pleasant surroundings of our Egypts to travel toward the land of promise. It is a journey through the desert. It is a wilderness that has its cost. But the promise of becoming the people of God, both as individuals and as a body, is the call to step out in response to God's call.

It is lived within the tension of never having a home we can call our own; of being a wandering pilgrim people in this life. Our problems arise when we want to stop, settle down, pitch our tents, and live only within the assurances of yesterday's gains.

Community offers us the chance to be ourselves and encourages that growth in each of us which will allow us to be pilgrims into ever deeper dimensions of what it means to be called God's people. The most we can expect from community is not that everyone will be like us, but that, though they may not understand us, they allow and encourage us to be our true selves and to be true to our calling to discipleship. That is a great gift.

Meditation Exercises

For your meditation this week, work with 1 Corinthians 13. Again use the reflective reading processes outlined in chapter 1. Read it over several times, preferably in one of the modern translations and meditate on it by using four or five verses a day. On the next-to-last day, write out your own paraphrase of it. Say it verse-by-verse in your own words so it becomes your translation. Write all of this in your journal.

Then, as a guide for working with the dimensions of community for you, work a day or two in your journal with each of the following questions:

1. Look at your life up to the present and write down the *persons* who stand out in each period of your life to the present. Try to allow your mind to recall the earliest person, and then gradually bring it down to the present. These may have been persons who were kind or mean to you. Just try to recall the persons who in some way stand out in your past and present. Include family members as they stand out in particular periods of your life. Allow this to be a biography of your life as told through the persons you have encountered.

After you have constructed the *biography-through-significant-persons*, reflect back over it and star (*) the persons who *affirmed* you along the way. Try to remember how they affirmed you and *what* they affirmed about you. You might write down these things beside their names.

2. Who was the *most meaningful person* in your life: (1) during your pre-school years, ages birth–5; (2) ages 6–12; (3) adolescent years, ages 13–21; and (4) since? These are the persons who were the most important to you, the persons who blessed and affirmed you.

3. Draw a diagram of the *table where you ate the meals* with your family during the first eighteen years of your life. Place each of the family members around it as they sat, and put their names on those places. Draw the *lines of affirmation* that happened at that table. Who blessed and affirmed whom? Who withheld affirmation? Then, add the persons outside of that room (such as a close friend, a grandparent, aunt or uncle, or absent family member) who blessed the persons in that room. For instance, you may have been affirmed by a grandmother who was not present, and your mother by her father who had been dead for years.

4. If you were to ask *ten persons* to be community to you, who would you ask? Ask anyone who comes to your mind. What kinds of persons would they be? Would they be persons out of your past, persons in the present, persons at church, persons at work? Try to reflect on whether these are persons who are in authority, persons who are able to affirm and accept you, persons who wouldn't participate even if you would invite them to be your community, persons who have wounds and problems that they are dealing with—what kind of persons would you ask to be community to you?

Begin to consider five persons whom you might ask to become a support community on an on-going basis in your church now, and consider plans for your first meeting.

9

Engaged in Brokenness

The inner work of God is not a call to escape from persons or to flee the world with all its problems and brokenness. It is a call to see persons in a new light and to know the world with new eyes of reality.

As we begin to deal with the illusions within ourselves, we can begin to re-engage the world with its illusions. Now we see the points of relevance, as well as those comfortable points where formerly we played the game of witness and ministry. We see the depths of a wounded world and know that a ministry to its brokenness is a ministry of costliness and of sustained duration. One can't minister with a costly ministry by putting band-aids over festering wounds, or with once- or twice-a-year baskets of do-goodism.

It has been said that 'the party is over for western materialism and its way of thinking that it can consume most of the world's goods and ignore the inequities and needs of the majority of the world.' That seems to be a harsh statement, but slowly it is becoming a reality. No doubt historians will look back at this century and describe it as one in which the oppressed peoples of this world rose up to be free and demanded to share in its benefits.

Arnold Toynbee, several years ago in an address at Williamsburg, Virginia, on the continuing effects of the American Revolution, said:

> By now, the eighteenth-century American shot has indeed been heard all 'round the world. The Revolution has become world-wide and the Old World, as well as the

New World, is swarming with the American Revolution's progeny. The Russian, Chinese, Egyptian, Congolese, and Cuban revolutions display, unmistakably, their origins in the parent revolution in this country. . . . And I suggest that we can state, in terms of the revolutionary American generation, the issue—possibly the most crucial one in all subsequent American history—on which the American people has to come to a decision in our generation. What is going to be America's reaction to America's own revolution now that this American-inspired revolution has become world-wide? America's choice between her two alternative possible responses is going—I am sure—to be crucial for America's destiny, because it is going to decide what America's relations are to be with the majority of the human race.

This majority is revolutionary-minded today because it is suffering not only a political injustice of the kind that provoked eighteenth-century Americans into fighting the Revolutionary War. The majority today is suffering social and economic injustice as well. Two-thirds or three-quarters of mankind are now still living only just above the starvation line, and are still frequently dropping below it. Is America going to offer herself to this hungry majority as their leader? It is open to her to take the lead again in its present world-wide stage. And, if she decides to do this, she has it in her power to help these aspiring people to help themselves . . . Will the American people expend themselves and its spiritual and material resources on promoting this world-wide revolutionary enterprise? Or will America decide to take the alternative course? Will she concentrate her efforts on trying to preserve the vested interests of the affluent minority of the human race? Will she take, as her measure of success, the quantity, per head, of material goods consumed at home, instead of measuring her success by the quantity of fundamental material and spiritual needs that she can help the still indigent majority of mankind to satisfy?

This is the question that is confronting America today. And this, I believe, involves for America the supreme question of to be or not to be. If America does take the lead in the American-born world revolution of our time, then she will continue to march in the van of mankind along the main high road of human destiny. On the other hand, if she were to make the great refusal, she would be side-tracking herself. She would be inviting destiny to pass her by. Indeed, she would be giving destiny no other choice. For, if America were to refuse to play this role, a dozen other lands would be vying with each other to snatch it. Russia and China would perhaps be the obvious first candidates in the field.

But why should America think of rejecting a role that is so obviously her manifest destiny? She might reject it for the reason that moved the young man with great posses-sions to go away sorrowful from his encounter with Jesus. The young man failed to bring himself to fulfil the condi-tion on which Jesus was willing to accept him as His follower. He could not bring himself to sell all that he had and give it to the poor.[1]

For the Christian these words of Toynbee's have a sting, especially those of us in Western Christianity. In the United States, for example, we have in the last thirty years built more church buildings than at any other time in our history. And still we continue to spend ninety to ninety-five per cent of all religious gifts and contributions on ourselves, while the agenda of the world is human dignity, hunger, survival and equality. Unless we begin to 'see things as they really are' and ask 'Why not?' we may find that American Christianity, along with the nation, has sold its soul for a mess of pottage.

The disciple of Christ cannot ignore the agenda of human need in the world. We may despair with assistance programmes at home and overseas, but we can never despair of our brothers and sisters as long as they are in need. We can never divert our eyes from human suffering and tragedy to soft carpets, an expensive organ, and a good programme. The follower of Christ is immersed in the brokenness without being overwhelmed. She stands there in the gap of human need and stays.

The message is clearly written; the world is not going to be organized in the future as it has been in the past. The follower of Christ is the first to understand that. She knows that brokenness cries out for healing and wholeness, and she becomes one of those who stands alongside of the oppressed and suffering. She sees and understands the real agenda of the world, though, as part of the privileged, it also is costly for her to step out of that position into one that 'gives a cup of cool water in Jesus' name'.

The world's agenda includes a cry for equality and freedom. It seeks to be free from oppression, no matter how long it takes and how many obstacles have to be overcome. The media have shown them that there is another way of life possible, and they want it now. As Toynbee also said:

> The world's peasantry has now waked up to a realization of the possibility that their conditions of life can be changed for the better—and changed at least partly by their own action. This is a revolutionary change of outlook. For these peasants have never dreamed before of what they are dreaming of now. They have been living in a state of resignation since the date, some five thousand years ago, when their patient shoulders were first saddled with the load of civilization whose amenities, up till now, have been a privileged minority's monopoly.[2]

The follower of Christ in the Western world today, in the midst of brokenness, has several roles to play. First of all, as one who is the recipient of the gifts of Western society, he has a duty to share those gifts with others. The gifts of human dignity, adequate food, shelter, education and the freedoms that accompany them are gifts of God. The burning question is, 'Why, O Lord, have we received these gifts and not others?' That same question was the central issue for Israel. 'Why, Lord, have you chosen little, insignificant Israel to reveal yourself to, and not the other mighty nations of the world?' The answer to that question for Israel, as it is today for Western Christianity, is that we are not more deserving than the rest. Many of us think that we have worked harder than others and, therefore, deserve more. Too many others have also toiled all of their lives and have never received one-tenth of what we have.

It is not because it is our inalienable right. It is also theirs, and they have received nothing! Do we have a God who is capricious in His giving; rights for one and not rights for others? Neither is it because we are mightier and more powerful, and to the victor go the spoils. Many before us, and even now, are as powerful, and they have not been equally blessed.

No, the only reason we have been blessed, as God told Abraham and the nation of Israel, is that we may bless others—'I will bless you in order that you might become a blessing to others' (Gen. 12.2). Paul echoed these words to the church at Corinth: 'And God is able to give you more than you need, so that you will always have all you need for yourselves and more than enough for every good cause. He will always make you rich enough to be generous at all times' (2 Cor. 9.8,11, GNB).

It is reported that a man one time came to Gandhi complaining about a financial injustice that a person had done him and wanting Gandhi to tell the other person to give him his money. Gandhi's advice was, 'Reduce your wants, and you will be able to supply your needs.' Our wants make us vulnerable. By reducing our wants, we reduce our vulnerability to the capriciousness of supply. Readjusting our wants requires a decision on our part to look for a new means of valuing what really is necessary. Then we will have more than enough to exercise our ministry of privilege. We have been privileged, not to be the sole consumers of our privilege, but to be the generous sharers of our unique inheritance in the world.

Thus ours is the role of sharer of those gifts. The early missionaries understood this. As they went, they carried the gifts of emerging, industrial nations. Sometimes their gifts were given wrongly, and sometimes the gifts they carried were inferior to the civilizations they uprooted in the process. Yet, the gifts of education, medicine, the raised status of women, the care of the rejected persons of society, and the easing of the cost of toiling for one's bread through improved methods—all were given as genuine gifts to a world that continues to benefit from them. These were gifts compatible with the good news of Jesus Christ they proclaimed.

Today, we still stand as the sharers of technological gifts to humankind to help them in making life more dignified, enabling millions, not just the privileged few, to realize their potential, rather than spending all of life trying to satisfy the basic needs of food, clothing, shelter, and safety. Still many of our gifts of a technological society are more harmful than good, but our capacity to feed, clothe, educate, heal, care, and solve problems could more than compensate for the continuing suffering of the broken parts of humankind.

Second, as recipients of God's unmerited blessings and as those who know what could and should be, but also know that the 'not yet' of technological progress remains beyond the reach of the majority of the world's millions for many generations to come, we are to be those who stand in the gaps of suffering and brokenness and incarnate caring and hope. We are those who offer a cup of water in Jesus' name in the meantime. We are to be where suffering humanity will never know adequate meals, houses, education, and hospitals. We are to stand there, engulfed by the seas of suffering and 'take it' and 'take it' over and over again, all the time knowing that there is a way to do something about it.

But because of the sinfulness of humankind—political dealings and bureaucracies, our willingness to do it only if it is profitable, or our attitude of superiority which says, 'If they would help themselves, they could do something about it'—nothing is done. And the followers of Christ are there and know better, but have to live with the questioning faces of the suffering which cry out, 'Why?' We are the 'ministers in the gaps of human suffering' until humankind is willing to 'give the cup of cold water'.

Mother Teresa doesn't make sense in Calcutta, India. There are just too many dying, starving, rejected masses in that city for her 'to do any good'. Why not just give up? You can't change the system that produces those castaways! She stays because every person is valuable, and until the world changes the system, someone must be there to help.

Albert Schweitzer operated out of what many felt was an outdated, outmoded hospital in the heart of Gabon because of his own belief in a 'reverence for life'. He explained that he had found his simple motive for going in the parable of Lazarus and the rich man, Dives (Luke 16.19–31). He identified Dives, endowed with all the benefits of culture and science, with the white man, and Lazarus with the Negro, exploited and oppressed and lacking even medical treatment. So he took a medical degree and prepared himself to spend the rest of his life in the gaps of suffering.

Clarence Jordan on a farm in Americus, Georgia, trying to live out the experiment of Christian brotherhood between blacks and whites, was shot at, cursed, and turned out of his local Southern Baptist church. Why did he persist? Because he had to take his place in the gaps between possibility and actuality.

Gordon Cosby, in a congregation tiny by numerical standards, among other ministries in that church, seeks to provide for the housing needs of the poor in Washington, D.C. Some wonder what ten or twelve apartment buildings do to relieve the suffering of thousands living in rat-infested unheated slums where physical life is cheap and threatened constantly. But the gaps have to have someone who incarnates the meaning of the paschal mystery of victory by taking the world's suffering on to themselves. 'Jubilee Housing' is one of those ministries which stands in the gaps of human suffering today.

In the third place, we as Western Christians can be a 'sign of Presence' to the promise of faith, hope, and love. Because we are there, we point beyond to an eschatological meaning that is not completely found in the present suffering. We become those who can see over the horizons and know the hope of another dimension. We are aware that history is just part of God's story. His working out of His purposes transcends historical circumstances. We are those who have already begun to participate in it through a saving relationship in Jesus Christ.

Our presence becomes God's presence. Though we are not presumptuous to say that we perfectly incarnate the Word of God, nevertheless, we are an incarnation. We are a witness, a testimony, to God's working out of His purposes. This is what witnessing is all about. We are a witness to faith, hope, and love. It is not just a verbal witness, but a living witness to the truth of faith, hope, and love in Christ. It is an 'as you go' making of disciples to Jesus, because of the incarnation of that faith, hope, and love. It is a ministry to brokenness that includes not only the physical, emotional and intellectual suffering, but the spiritual suffering as we call persons to wholeness in Jesus.

As presence and sign, we are also prophetic. We see over the horizon and know what could be and point to it. Because of the disturbance to the status quo, we know the tension of straining towards the future while standing in the present moment. We know the guilt and anger that such a prophetic stance calls up, but that is part of the cost of a prophetic witness.

Finally, as Western Christians we are those who are living between the times. And we are called to be a gift on behalf of all of the body of Christ to the brokenness wherever we are. We are called to be a sign of the whole Body of Christ, not just one segment of it. There is an inward togetherness about our presence there at the point of brokenness, as if all of those who claim 'Jesus is Lord' were there. Time is too short and the urgency too great for us to continue to afford the luxury of a Christianity that refuses to call one part of the body, brother and sister in Christ. It will take the work of the entire body to make even a dent in this world's brokenness.

We are there out of the gifts of ourselves, not out of guilt. We are at the points of brokenness because we know those are the places we need to be in order for us to be complete. We have sensed that call as 'good news' for us. No *ought, should, have-to*, or *must* keeps us there. True, there are times when it is difficult, but what keeps us there is choice, not duty. We are there because we have responded to the call of Christ. That is our place of ministry and witness in order for us to be who we are, not because we have been forced to stay.

Our call is to be a radically obedient people of God. We are to be a people who have lived deeply enough to see the reality of the brokenness of the world we live in, yet a people who have not been overwhelmed by it. We are to be a people who have responded by living life in the gaps of brokenness through a sustained ministry and witness which incarnates the faith, hope, and love of Jesus Christ to humanity's masses. We have dealt with the redevelopment of our own lives and adopted an economic life-style of sufficiency, 'enough', so we can be involved in a living witness to what God is doing in the reconciliation of all humankind to Himself.

We are to be a light when the collapse comes. We have been called to get ready by knowing how to live deeply in Christ and to call others to Him. We are those who have identified ourselves with the oppressed, crushed, disen-franchised of the world—even though we know that we are part of the oppressors. We are those who have lived so long as the imperial, privileged few, but who now renounce our rights to status in order to call all of those who follow Christ to a new and deeper life of ministry and witness. We stand on the side of a theology of liberation, rather than a theology of oppression, and say with Jesus,

> The Spirit of the Lord is upon me,
>   because he has chosen me to
>   bring good news to the poor.
> He has sent me to proclaim
>   liberty to the captives
>   and recovery of sight to the
>   blind;
> to be set free the oppressed
>   and to announce that the time
>   has come
>   when the Lord will save his
>   people.
>   (Luke 4.18–19 GNB)

Meditation Exercises

This week in your meditations, work with either one or both of these passages from Matthew's Gospel: 5.3–16 or 25.31–46, using again the process outlined in chapter 1. As you work with these spend an equal amount of time scanning the headlines of the newspaper. In your journal, write whatever impressions you have as you work with the Scriptures. Then copy the five or six major headlines from the newspaper alongside those impressions each day. Karl Barth said this was how he did effective Bible study. Allow the two to interact with each other and set up for you a dialogue between these two sources. These become the 'Liturgy of the Word' for you each day of this week.

10
You Don't Have to
Die on Every Cross

'For to him who has will more be given, and he will have abundance' (Matt. 13.12, RSV). 'Close the windows, I've seen too much! I can't stand to see any more. It's too much. My eyes hurt, and I hurt down deep inside. If I see any more, it will kill me!'

That becomes the cry of anyone who asks to see the great needs of society in all of its brokenness. When we were asking to see things just a little clearer, to see God's will for our lives, we were dealing with the matter of the capacity to see. Now we must deal with an entirely new set of questions. This is the way God works with us. He uses one set of questions, which we ask at one period in our life, to lead us to that point in which we begin to ask an entirely different set of questions. This is how he leads us onward towards continuing growth.

What we are dealing with now is the crisis of our finitude. We frankly can't do all that we see. The person who says, 'I don't know where to minister,' may be saying, 'I don't see,' or 'I don't know what to do.' But, the person who is dealing with her finitude anxiety is saying, 'Out of all this that is around me to be done, how can I possibly do it all?' The overwhelming need all around us begins to crush us and our temptation is to give up in desperation. There's just too much to do, and the magnitude of the task is such that we couldn't possibly make a dent in the need. So the easiest thing for us to do is to give up, to simply say, 'It can't be done.' 'The poor you will always have with you,' said Jesus (Matt. 26.11), so let's stop fretting about it.

That is one possible solution. To give up. To resolve our inner conflict about the fact that we can't do it all, by saying, 'I am finite, so I'm going to forget trying to do anything about it.'

Another solution, in our activistic society, is to assume that we can do everything we see that needs to be done. That has its trap, too. We start doing one thing, then another, and finally, we are doing everything that we see needs to be done, or anything that anyone thinks up. We do it out of the inner compulsion that assumes, 'If I don't do it, it won't get done.'

Both solutions are in error. When we give up, we assume that God is not working anywhere else with that concern in His universe and that we will have to do whatever will be done in our own strength. The second error assumes that we are as God and can minister to every need that we see. We assume somehow that we are the only minister God has; if we don't do it, He will not get it done. Both solutions assume that God is not at work in His universe, and both assume that human effort alone somehow is the only answer to the problems of the universe. Both have failed to see that our task is to co-operate with grace in the work that God is already doing in His universe.

Gordon Cosby first helped me identify my feelings that everything depended on me through his description of 'finitude anxiety' that assumed I had to do it all. A phrase from Thomas Kelly has continued to help me resolve this problem that I was dealing with. Kelly said that this world was too vast and a lifetime was too short for me to assume that I could carry all responsibilities. He said that God 'does not burden us equally with all things, but considerately puts upon each of us just a few central tasks, as emphatic responsibilities.'[1] He concluded, 'We cannot die on *every* cross, nor are we expected to.'[2]

Both of these men have described the problem that we all have to deal with as we begin to see reality all around us and struggle with our capacities to deal with it. It is the problem of focus. Where previously we asked to see, now we deal with the problem of focusing that which we see.

Too often, rather than dealing with the particularization of our responsibility, the problem of focus, we settle for 'doing good, moral, religious things'. There is nothing wrong with them. They are morally good within themselves, but they are not *our focus*. Jesus had several warnings to the people of his day about just doing 'good things', rather than doing those things for which 'call' became a focusing of responsibility.

No more dramatic account of the focusing of responsibility is found than in the reply of the man who said he would follow Jesus but had to first go and bury his father. Jesus' reply seems insensitive: 'Follow me, and leave the dead to bury their dead' (Matt. 8.22, NEB). The urgency of the call of Christ was such that he was saying to the man, 'If you follow me you must leave off those good religious practices, such as a son's duty in staying at home until the death of his father, and come follow me.' What the son wanted to do was to fulfil his religious obligation first and then follow the specific call. Jesus' reply was: 'If you think that you can avoid the focusing of responsibility now by playing around with religious duties, you have not heard the urgency and unconditional nature of the call!'

Jesus was saying that if one had only heard at the level of fulfilling religious obligations then that one should go on and take care of the religious obligations of burying the dead. But, if one had heard the claims of His call at another level, then it would demand that that one would have to refocus his responsibilities and duties. Many a missionary has been faced with this same internal dilemma: to stay home and fulfil the religious obligations of honouring father and mother by being there in their old age and seeing that the final rites of burial were taken care of or to follow the deep claims of Christ and refocus that call.

This is not a matter of being insensitive to human need, for each person has to answer the question of focus in his own way under the leadership of the Holy Spirit. It is a particularization of responsibility, believing that in the economy of God there are enough gifted people to take care of all that needs to be done—if each one would live out of the particular focus. This is not a problem just for missionaries. It is a problem that everyone faces as he hears God's call to deeper levels of *followship*, not being content with just doing religious things. In the economy of God's plan, there could be a focused person for every need that has to be done. And, the temptation to just do 'good, moral, religious things' becomes an avoidance of focus.

God does not leave us helpless in this dilemma of focus. He has given us two tools for focus: vision and spiritual gifts. The problem of abundance, of seeing too much, is dealt with through a vision of what could be, and spiritual gifts are given to accomplish that end. Very often it means a reordering of priorities in our lives. It means a rearranging of life itself. But, the priceless treasure that is to be found is to be able to know that what we are doing is uniquely our calling and seeing the little that we do multiplied as the loaves and fishes. Then we become deeply aware that in our being focused, God is not talking about our being brilliant. That may be, too. But, He is once again taking our little bit and making it accomplish much. He takes the weak and confounds the strong.

If there are two additional illnesses which keep us from being focused in the West, they are the pollution of opportunity and its consequence, unexamined activity. We exist in a society where there is an over-abundance of things to do.

There is always someone to sell us on their cause, their programme, their new activity. And, we succumb to it without examining it in relationship to the uniqueness of our lives. Focus causes us to have to deal with all the activities that want us to 'dance when they dance' or call us a wet blanket when we don't. We have to examine our involvements in order to become focused persons who have centred down in all of our involvements, even religious involvements.

The importance of images, visions, symbols, or signs for human kind has been the concern of scholarly interest in recent years. Probably the work of Carl Jung is as well known in this area as anyone. Whereas Sigmund Freud had said that drives become the source for centralizing psychic energy, Jung said that psychic energy gets centralized around certain symbols, images, or visions. Ira Progoff, one of the best interpreters of Jung and his work, said that symbols refer to something that is relatively unknown, so, therefore, a symbol does not stand for something known, as a sign would. He further pointed out,

> The characteristic of the symbol is that it opens beyond itself, touching in the form of a representation something that the understanding does not fully encompass, but into which it wishes to reach. . . . It is a direct, continuing experience of something real, which is yet indefinable for Man, and in itself is in need of signs in order that its presence may be communicated.[3]

Thus a symbol, or a vision, is an unconscious and intuitive way of reaching out to a reality that otherwise could not be known. But it is real. It is a 'living thing' for the person and becomes a means for her to 'know' an inward reality in a powerfully new way. Progoff says that the symbol 'comes' to the individual; it cannot be consciously developed and rationally worked out. It comes out of the unconscious and becomes a living reality which gives life a new orientation and a channel through which energy is released.

Jung said that these images, symbols, or visions are in us, and their function is to gather up and channel our psychic energies for some useful action. If symbols and visions are used properly, they do something to us. They release us and a power flows. But if they are not functioning, we feel upset, fretful, and can't get things going within us. According to Jung when this happens the symbol has become a 'dead symbol'. It no longer functions as the integrating core of life for us.

For Paul, the most powerful symbol, he called it a vision, was the one that he experienced on the road to Damascus. It is referred to three times in the book of Acts (9.1 ff.; 22.6–16; 26.12–18) and five other places in his letters (1 Cor. 9.1; 15.8; 2 Cor. 12.1 ff.; Gal. 1.13 ff.; Phil. 3.6). In defending himself before King Agrippa, after he had told of the experience of the blinding light, the falling off his horse, the voice from heaven, and the resultant blindness, he said, 'And so, King Agrippa, I did not disobey the vision I had from heaven. First in Damascus and in Jerusalem and then in the whole country of Israel and among the Gentiles, I preached that they must repent of their sins and turn to God, and do the things that would show they had repented' (Acts 26.19, GNB).

What vision was Paul talking about? The Damascus conversion experience? The sight of Jesus? The vision which Paul received that day was the vision of a Gentile mission. The message of that vision is told us in the message given to Ananias: 'Go, because I have chosen him to serve me, to make my name known to Gentiles and kings, and to the people of Israel' (Acts 9.15, GNB). Later, in his defence after his arrest in the Temple, Paul told of the confirmation of the Damascus vision in a second vision he had in the Temple. In that second vision, God told him to leave the work of trying to witness to the Jews for an exclusive mission to the Gentiles (Acts 22.17–21).

To equate vision solely with seeing pictures, as in an ecstatic trance, is to miss the point. If we simply wait for some ecstatic experience to grab us, we may miss the impact of what happened to Paul. Not everyone is going to be struck down with a blinding light on the Damascus Road. But, very often the power of an 'inbreaking moment', the sudden flash of insight which enables us to see everything in a perspective that we've never seen before, becomes a way of releasing us, and energy begins to flow. Paul after Damascus was as energetic, and maybe more so, in working with the vision of a Gentile mission as he had been before Damascus in persecuting the followers of Jesus. The symbol of the ministry of reconciliation to the Gentiles was revolutionary, and it became the basis for the new thrust of Christianity. It captured Paul and became the way of refocusing his life.

When we ask for a Damascus road experience we are really asking, not for a cataclysmic salvation experience, but for the focused vision of what God would have us do with our lives. We are asking to be focused.

Jesus was focused. His reading of Isaiah 61.1–2 in the synagogue of Nazareth (Luke 4.16 ff.) focused His mission. That was the vision He had of His ministry so that when John the Immerser asked if He were really the Messiah, Jesus said, 'Go back and tell John what you have seen and heard'. He used the same language of the Isaish passage to describe His work to John (Luke 7.22, GNB).

Vision is God's gift to us to help us live with our finitude, to enable us to deal with our particular responsibilities amid the over-abundance of opportunity, to help us begin to deal with our unique, true selves. Vision is that bringing together, at an intuitive level, of the gathered-up fragments of our lives and refocusing them in a mission of reconciliation with God.

Visions cause us to channel all of our energies into a certain direction, and they predispose us to receive God's gifts to us in a particular kind of ministry. They allow us to begin focusing our lives in certain directions and to receive the work of God in more particular directions.

Elizabeth O'Connor reported Gordon Cosby's vision for what has become known as one of the most influential churches in America today, the Church of the Saviour in Washington, D.C. As a young military chaplain in Europe, he had a vision of a new kind of church in America:

> In those incredible moments when bread was broken and Christ stood in their midst, Gordon committed himself to being the minister of an unknown church that would be ecumenical in its spirit, in dialogue with all the churches—indeed with all men. . . . In their youthful enthusiasm it seemed to them both that such a church would surely be empowered by the Spirit and infuse with its life the whole of Christendom.[4]

That is the vision that has animated his spirit for nearly forty years.

Mother Teresa said that in 1946 on the train that was carrying her to her annual spiritual retreat she experienced the vision 'to give up all and follow him into the slums to serve him among the poorest of the poor'.[5] So, she walked out of the lovely girls' school to work among the rejected poor and dying of the slums of Calcutta.

Teilhard de Chardin, amid the despair of the trenches in World War I, affirmed that God did not intend His creation to end up committing suicide. There emerged in him the vision of a creation that was proceeding from God and returning to God as something finer than it began.[6] His sharing of that vision through twelve books has given modern persons a vision that makes sense out of the chaotic meaninglessness of our time.

Clarence Jordan, in the post-depression years in the inner city of Louisville, Kentucky, and as the first director of missions of the Long Run Baptist Association, saw the despair of poor, rural blacks being pushed off the farms of the South, into the crowded urban ghettos of the North looking for hope. Jordan's vision was of a farm that would be started in the South, where he could help these people find fruitful lives on the farms. Clarence 'believed in the concept of community, and he had the free spirit and courage it took to pursue the dream of peace and brotherhood into the Deep South'.[7] That vision became Koinonia Farms in Americus, Georgia, a radical experiment in brotherhood in the South.

Not all visions are that dramatic, nor have to be. It may be nothing more than a vision of helping the hungry in a city, the providing of inner city housing for the poor, work with the mentally handicapped, or a response to a plea for help as a big brother. What happens in each case, though, is that each one becomes energized and focused through an inner vision.

Rollo May has described some of the elements of the process vision takes.[8] An inner vision is our encounter with our world. It is our emotional and intellectual involvement with it. There is an encounter with it, and in our struggle to make sense out of it we begin to use our imagination to construct new forms and relationships in it. We seek an inner consistence with what is going on both consciously and below the level of our conscious awareness. Thus, an 'insight' is born almost spontaneously, and we 'see' with a clarity that we've not seen before. An inner integration takes place that causes us to feel that 'everything is right in the world', and a new thing is born.

The process may happen something like this. There is a suddenness of illumination which may even be opposite to all of the theories we have clung to. But, all of a sudden, everything becomes vivid, and we feel an immediate certainty of rightness about it all. The new fits into the pattern of previous inner commitments and helps us 'fill in the missing gaps', so that we see it as a new whole. Finally, we discover that this insight came to us after we had had a long period of activity in working on the problem, and then began to relax our inner controls; there was an alternation between our own efforts and relaxation—it just 'came to us'.

This may sound like a process of irrationality. It is true that this dimension produces an anxiety in us because in seeing new possibilities, we also destroy something previously held. But, the risk is to see the vision of the new possibility, to let go of the securities and resistance, and become engaged in the passionate reforming of our world. The risk is the risk of inner tensions as we are involved in the process.

Yet, it is also a healing experience as we come to discover in the dialogue between spontaneity and the form, within which the vision takes shape, a limiting process which is also healing. As May points out, those who err on the side of all spontaneity risk the psychotic destruction of not being able to make sense out of the bombardment of possibilities. While those who err on the side of form risk the staleness of only the forms given to us in the past. Vision is the gift of God for our co-creation with Him in making sense out of the world and allowing things to be seen as they can be. It allows our potentiality to become actualized. It allows us to join Him in mission.

Therefore, within the concept of vision, we begin to understand 'spiritual gifts' and calling. Our being gifted persons, endowed by God to join Him in the mission of reconciliation in our own unique way, becomes focused as we start to see possibility in the struggle to know what we uniquely bring to the accomplishment of that vision. Not all visions are ours, nor are all gifts ours. As we become focused, we face our finiteness, knowing that in God's economy that is all right. But we do have to deal with that 'cross' that is uniquely ours, the one that releases us to be ourselves. It is in that creative act of dealing with our 'spiritual gifts' and the vision that has been given to us that we experience what it is to live out of the true self, the one gifted in Christ. Then we can understand the words of Augustine Baker: 'Mind your call, it's your all in all.'

Meditation Exercises

This week in your quiet time, there will be several different exercises aimed at helping you deal with your *gifts* and the *vision* that unifies and focuses your life.

1. *The first day* will help you deal with the unfolding of your life up to the present. In your journal, using a 'timeline', mark it off into the four or five *major divisions* of your life (for example, childhood, high school, military service, got married, children, college, jobs, death of a relative, or retirement). Then add the three or four events that were the *turning points* that have shaped your life the most (a job offer, death, etc.) and indicate them on the timeline by stars (*). After you have constructed your timeline, write out a sentence or two about each area you divided it into, and elaborate on the turning points in your life.

2. *The second day*—take the most recent period from the timeline you constructed yesterday and elaborate on it by adding the following elements to it:

   a. Mark it off in terms of when it began (months and year) to the present.

   b. Run it over in the screen of your mind. What inward images or feelings come to you immediately? Relax, not trying to think of it; let it emerge as you run that period over in your mind. Write the word(s) down.

c. Now start filling in the details of the most recent period: What *events* began the period? Was it a specific idea or decision you made? If not, write 'none'. Write down the names of all *persons* who stand out during this period (those involved in good as well as discomforting experiences). Name the activities you were involved in during this period. What *hopes and difficulties* did you experience during this period? Were there events and *experiences* that dramatically changed the course of your life? How were you *feeling* physically and emotionally during this period? Were there any *unusual coincidences* during this period?

d. Write two or three adjectives to describe this period and write one sentence to describe it, beginning with the words, 'It was like . . .'

3. *The third day*—Meditate on Acts 3.1–10. Use the process described in chapter 1, except when you come to 'ponder'. Then answer these three questions instead:

a. When asked for something we did not have, many times we experienced one of the following feelings: frustration, embarrassment, anger, desire to ignore him, the other person, or some other feeling. Which do you suppose came first to Peter and John?

b. Describe the expression you 'saw' on the face of the man when Peter and John told him they could not give him what he asked for.

c. What did his face 'say' after they gave him what they had—the gift of healing?

d. Where are you being asked to give when you don't have anything to give?

e. What, instead, do you have to give that could turn your whole life in a new direction?

4. *The fourth day*—Answer the following questions, not with words, but by *drawing figures* or *symbols* to represent

your answers (you may elaborate on the symbols later in your journal if you wish, so you do not forget what the representations meant to you at this time): First, relax; close your eyes and begin to think about things you have accomplished in your lifetime. When you are ready, open your eyes and begin *drawing* your responses to the following statements:

a. Name an accomplishment in each of these periods of your life: ages 1–14; 15–25; 26–35; 36–50; 51–65; 65–present.

b. Name an accomplishment of the last twelve months.

c. Name three things you like to do.

d. How are you creative; where does your imagination work the strongest?

e. If you could make something that would change the course of the world, what would it be?

f. Name three words you would like to be remembered by.

5. For the *remaining days* this week, work the following questions in your journal:

a. What is your gift? Name it.

b. What is your call? Try to write it out in one sentence.

c. What vision do you have for allowing God's work to be done more effectively where you are?

d. If there were no limitations of time, money, education, or circumstance, and you could do anything in the world you wanted to, what would it be? Pay attention to the images and inner visions you have as you use your imagination here.

e. As you watch yourself do this thing, what special gifts and talents would you need to do it?

f. What risks and what rewards would be involved? What would you have to do to work with God in making that happen?

11

Empowered

Our call to engage in a ministry of reconciliation with God to the brokenness of the world is a call to walk into that brokenness in the same manner Jesus did, and with the same life-style that guided Him and the disciples after Him. Ours is to minister and witness out of powerlessness and as servants. Then we will be accessible to the power of God through His Holy Spirit in all that we do. To be empowered means to co-operate with God's grace through the work of His Holy Spirit.

The Gospel writers report that people were constantly amazed at the ministry and teaching of Jesus because it had power and authority (Mark 1.22, Luke 4.36–37). When Jesus sent out the twelve (Luke 9.1–6) and later the seventy-two (Luke 10:1 ff.), He gave His disciples power and authority for their ministry.

Ours is a society that talks a great deal about power and authority. We speak of it in terms of: How much do you possess? How much do you produce? How much money do you earn? Who do you know? What position do you occupy? Yet, this was not the kind of power that Jesus was talking about with His disciples. He was not speaking of power in the usual way. This became a source of misunderstanding among the disciples who expected Him to be the forceful liberator of their nation. Though they recognized a power and authority about Him which was different from that of their own religious leaders and rulers, they had difficulty understanding the source of it.

We will find ourselves making the same mistake and

assuming that our work, ministry, and life are to be lived in one dimension when Jesus is asking us to live it in another.

To understand the power and authority which Jesus is talking about, we have to re-read the temptation story of Jesus. There we see how He faced several possible uses of power and authority and rejected them all in favour of one that was more appropriate to His mission. The three temptations (Matt. 4.1–11; Luke 4.1–13) were: (1) to turn stones into bread, (2) to jump off the highest place on the Temple of Jerusalem, and (3) to accept the gift of the rulership of the nations of the world.

First, in each of these three temptations, Jesus refused to accomplish His mission of making persons whole by one particular means of recognized power and authority. In the first instance, He refused to make persons obligated to Him by giving them the basic necessities of life (satisfying basic physiological needs), as humanitarian as that would have been. He re-stated the principle that food, though a basic necessity for sustaining life, was not the only basis of life sustenance. God's word was also necessary for living.

Second, Jesus rejected the power that comes when you simply 'dazzle' people. Jesus' basic gift (charisma) was that He was the Son of God. For that reason the angels would have protected Him had He jumped from the Temple's heights. Jesus, however, refused to use the power of 'signs and wonders' to attract people. He was constantly saying to persons, 'Keep this healing to yourself.' He did not want a kingdom built on the fading power of having to produce a bigger and better show each day. This appeals to those who want to see the latest and most bizarre, the newest fad. But, you can't build a kingdom on that kind of power. It won't last.

Third, Jesus rejected the power of political influence. He would not establish His kingdom as a ruler of nations. That power is the power of external authority and is based on someone having to lose. It is an authority of win/lose, over/ under, do them/before they do you. Jesus said to the disciples that this was not to be their way of doing business (Luke 22.25–26); they were, like Him, to take the form of a servant.

The Suffering Servant of Isaiah (Isa. 53) was to be the model for fulfilling the mission of Jesus, and He taught it to His disciples. He said, 'The chief of you [must become] like a servant' (Luke 22.26, NEB). Johannes Metz summarized the temptation story of Jesus as an enticement to accomplish His mission out of strength: 'Satan's temptation calls upon Jesus to remain strong like God, to stand within a protecting circle of angels, to hang on to his divinity (Phil. 2.6).'[1] Instead, Jesus chose the way of powerlessness.

This is seen in the way Jesus instructed His disciples about their ministry. If it sounds strange to our ears, it is because we are so enmeshed in the system of power-seeking, power- trading, power-brokering, and power-utilization that we see what Jesus said through eyes that consider Jesus naive and incredulous.

Jesus told the disciples to *lead from weakness*, not strength. This is seen in the sending of the twelve and the seventy-two (Matt. 9.35 to 10.16; Luke 10.1–16). He sent them out without a back-up team to feed, clothe and house the group, and then told the disciples to take no provisions themselves. Their dependence was to be on God's provision and the persons to whom they ministered. Jesus told Peter to put up his sword—thus exposing Himself to capture by those wanting to kill Him (John 18.10). And it is from Jesus Himself that we learn the most about leading from weakness rather than strength. Paul said that He 'made himself nothing, assuming the nature of a slave' (Phil 2.7, NEB). Jesus did not make it in His own strength, but made Himself vulnerable by letting go. Paul's testimony was that Jesus had said to him, 'My power is strongest when you are weak' (2 Cor. 12.9, GNB).

Jesus taught that from *unpromising beginnings* a new force is released. Jesus' own life on earth had begun that way, as a tiny baby in Bethlehem. He illustrated it with the parable of the mustard seed (Matt. 13.31–32). He showed how God packed a tree into that tiny seed, and though it had an unpromising beginning, it had a glorious end. He illustrated from this that God takes the small and makes it big.

In the same vein, Jesus told the disciples that God *takes the weak and confounds the strong*. From a handful of ordinary people, He fashioned one of the most powerful forces in the world. They were no intellectual threat to anyone. They were the rejects. But Jesus revealed the mysteries of the kingdom to the simple (Luke 10.21). They were not numerically superior. Nor were they to be feared as rich men of influence. They were nobodies. They had been ignored by all who ruled in that day and time. But they became the ones who overthrew—with a new kind of power— the Roman rule, the Jewish rule, and all the powerful, influential people of their day. Their martyrs' blood became the fear of all who ruled.

Jesus also *took the few and multiplied them* to do what was needed. As He had done with the loaves and fishes (Matt. 14.13 ff.), He took what was available, blessed it and multiplied it. And it became sufficient for the need at hand, with abundance left over. He took twelve and changed the world. He took those who could really hear, though many had followed Him, and like Gideon before Him, was able to accomplish much.

He taught them that they *had enough resources* and not to be anxious about the provisions of basic necessities for tomorrow (Matt. 6.25 ff.). He said that God knew them and would see that they were taken care of at that time. He even taught that they were to make that sort of request daily for bread (Matt. 6.11).

They were to *renounce all legitimate defences* (Matt. 5.38 ff.) by turning the other cheek. And, when they were rejected, they were simply to leave (Matt. 10.14).

They were to *forgive all persons their debts* (Matt. 6.12) and to love their enemies (Matt. 5.43 ff.). They were not to ask for vindication and punishment by God, because they belonged to Him and would await the judgement of the last days (Matt. 13.24 ff.).

They were to be *pilgrims without a place to lay their heads* that they could call their own (Matt. 8.18 ff.).

Finally, they were told that in *dying they would live*, and in losing their lives they would find them (Matt. 10.38–39; 16.25 ff.). Jesus said to them, 'If anyone wants to come with me, he must forget himself, carry his cross, and follow me' (Matt. 16.24, GNB).

This is not a picture of power as the world knows and exercises it. From the world's point of view, it is seen as powerlessness. It is the voluntary rejection of power in order to be 'empowered' as was Jesus in the role of a servant, even unto death on the cross. His was an obedience unto death that was free from a power-determined system, and in dying He allowed others to be set free from a power-dominated world. He called to Himself disciples who would demonstrate in their lives that they had been set free from the clutches of a power-dominated world and who could live life at a different level because of that freedom. Their only defence in the world power system were the arms Paul spoke of: truth, integrity, readiness to announce the good news of peace, faith, salvation, and the Word of God (Eph. 6.14–17).

This kind of power system demanded that people be truly free in order not to revert to older forms of power. There had to be an internal freedom that did not reach for the sword, the right contact, money, or a position of authority. What Jesus asked of them, and of us today, was, and is, to operate from a different power-base. It is the power-base of being 'empowered'.

From the position of powerlessness, we learn the accessibility of co-operating with the Holy Spirit who becomes our source of power. As Jesus sent out the twelve, He gave them power and authority (Luke 9.1). When the seventy-two returned, rejoicing about the power they had seen happen through them, He said again, 'I have given you the power' (Luke 10.19, NEB). As He taught the disciples about prayer, He said that the Father in heaven would give the Holy Spirit to those who asked Him (Luke 12.12). He told them that greater works would they do than He had done, because of His going and the coming of the Holy Spirit (John 14.12–16). Finally, after His resurrection, He told them to wait to receive the power of the Holy Spirit, which would enable them to be witnesses to the ends of the earth (Acts 1.8).

Obviously this power was compatible with their servant call, so it would be of a different sort of working than the power of the world. It would not be a power to overwhelm, pronounce final judgement, nor show who was boss! It would be the power that comes to those who have come to rest in God alone. It would be a power for those who had decided that they no longer trusted in their own self-sufficiency. It would be for those who had said they trusted God for their survival.

The Holy Spirit would be for those who no longer could rest in their own strength when the waters got rough. He would be there for those who are demonstrating the staying power of faith, hope and love in the most difficult situations.

The Holy Spirit would be for those whose ministry is to have a penetrating power like salt, light, and leaven. As such, they would be persons who live out of deeper resources than those that are available in superficial sources of power. They would live out of the nudgings of the Holy Spirit in their lives daily. They would no longer know the need to have to produce but only to co-operate with what God was already doing in his world. They would be, indeed, a charismatic people, for they would seek to be Spirit-controlled rather than controlled by the spirit of this world or the power of the false self. They would have access to a power that would allow them to be a people who were not dominated by having to force all their activity to happen—they could be a people who 'don't pump, but flow' as an artesian well.

We have to be taught by the Holy Spirit to know the deepest dimensions of this power, for we are so conditioned to work within the systems of power of this world that this language of Holy Spirit power seems strange to our ears. But the follower of Christ who is engaged in the brokenness of the world in a sustained ministry and witness soon finds out that she cannot minister and witness in her own power. She is asked by the Lord to 'let go', even as He had to do to be in touch with another source from which life can flow.

Some will think this is passivity. It is not. It is an active powerlessness in the power of the Holy Spirit. This is a self that seeks to be Spirit-directed, Spirit-controlled, and Spirit-taught, so one can know Jesus more intimately and co-operate with Him in ministry to the world. John Haughey said that there are two ways to follow Jesus. One of them is to follow Him in the relative security of the boat, where one can rest in numbers and a defined practice, although 'he might have to cope with the pervasive feeling that "we are not getting very far".' Or we could accompany Jesus out on the waves and let go to live life in the seemingly 'precarious, almost capricious element of the Spirit'. He concluded: 'A life of complete faith propels one to live not by his own ideas, impulses, or abilities, but by the leadings of the Spirit that

have much the same ebb and flow and unpredictability that
wind and waves do.'²

The church of privilege cannot let go. The person who
seeks to build life on status, money, degrees, muscle or
cunning cannot endure the powerlessness of the cross. It
becomes a scandal to intellectuals and blue-collar alike. This
type of power of Jesus seems like foolishness. But to the one
who seeks to follow Christ even deeper, the Spirit-controlled
life becomes the only way, for it was the way of the Lord.

Meditation Exercises

This week in your meditations, work with Romans 8.1–27.
In order to help you become aware of how you are involved in
power and how you use power and how power uses you, do
the following exercises in your journal:

1. Take the list of ten persons you made in chapter 8 and
arrange them in a priority order from one through ten. Keep
moving them around as you think they have *importance in the
group of ten*. Do this in pencil so you can erase and rearrange
them until you are satisfied. Now notice how you have
arranged them. What hidden dimensions of power are there
in the arrangement you have made? If that person in position
number one were to have arranged the group, would he have
put himself as number one? If so, why? This can help you
become aware of how people, even you, use power in posi-
tioning themselves in groups and informal gatherings.

2. The next time you are in a group of people (a meeting, a
business group, or a meeting of your group) draw a diagram
of how the conversation flows. Place lines from one person to
another as they talk, so you begin to have a diagram of how
the conversation is structured in that group. Now see if you
can determine from that diagram where the power is. Why is
it there? What is your role in that power? Do you take power,
yield it, use it, and why?

3. Become aware of how you use power in your ministry and witness. Do you try to overwhelm, intimidate, become an adversary to, prosecute, defend, acquiesce, avoid the other person's power, or use your physical presence over someone?

4. Concentrate on a releasing of world-dominated power, so you can be available to a Spirit-directed source of power. Be aware this week of the Holy Spirit's nudgings in your life. How is He 'making Himself available' to you? Are you responsive? If not, how could you become more sensitive to His nudgings? Note any times when you are experiencing a power in your ministry and witness that comes from the Holy Spirit. How could your life be lived more completely at that level? Do you notice any 'coincidences' in which you sense a co-operation with grace going on?

Record all of this in your journal.

12

Living Out of the Depths

Twice in the New Testament Paul speaks of the 'unsearchable riches' of Christ (Eph. 3.8; compare Rom. 11.33, KJV). Translators have commented that in both places the Greek language becomes complex as Paul begins to soar in his description of the deeper meanings of life in Christ. That Paul was a mystic has been acknowledged by many over the centuries. And, as many have found since, it is difficult to describe the unfathomable dimensions of God.

Paul said in Romans, 'How rich are the depths of God—how deep his wisdom and knowledge—and how impossible to penetrate his motives or understand his methods!' (Rom. 11.33, JB). And in Ephesians he said, 'To me, who am less than the least of all God's people, he has granted of his grace the privilege of proclaiming to the Gentiles the good news of the unfathomable riches of Christ, and of bringing to light how this hidden purpose was to be put into effect' (Eph. 3.8–9, NEB). In the first passage, the ecstatic words describe how God was going to redeem Israel ultimately, and in the second they speak of how God had been working out his purposes for the salvation of the Gentiles.

In both places Paul spoke of the 'depths of God' as being that dimension out of which God's ultimate purposes are revealed. Both passages attempt to describe the awe and wonder of becoming aware of the depths of God and seeing His purposes unfold.

Though God's ways are knowable, Paul could also marvel that the ways of God are much deeper, richer, and more unfathomable than seems apparent. Just because some things seem certain, we must remember that God's thoughts and ways are not ours. We cannot assume what God is thinking and then say, 'You must act as God has told me you should act.'

No, the depths of God are bottomless. They know no end. Thus, as we seek to become aware of God in our lives and want to live there, we come to realize with Paul that God's ways are both knowable and unfathomable. The person who seeks to know God intimately seeks to be more attentive to God in every way; yet His ways also elude us.

The writers of the spiritual classics referred to this intimate knowledge of God as 'union'. Many things were meant by the word. Some saw union with God as an experience in which a person literally 'stood outside of himself' in an experience of ecstasy. Paul said of his own experience, 'I know a man in Christ who, fourteen years ago, was caught up—whether still in the body or out of the body, I do not know; God knows—right into the third heaven. I do know, however, that this same person—whether in the body or out of the body, I do not know; God knows—was caught up into paradise and heard things which must not and cannot be put into human language' (2 Cor. 12.2–4, JB). Ecstasy, for many, may be too irrational for them to feel comfortable. Yet it has to be recognized as an element of union for some. However, it is not to be equated with union.

Others have referred to union as holiness and perfectionism, even others calling it a stage of 'sinless perfection'. The passage that is often cited to support this view is from Matthew: 'You, therefore, must be perfect, as your heavenly Father is perfect' (Matt. 5.48, RSV). However, it seems, in light of what the New Testament teaches elsewhere, that a stage of sinless perfection is not what is intended. What is intended by this passage and others in the New Testament is the pointing of persons towards the goal of spiritual maturity.

132

Just as the heavenly Father is holiness and spiritual maturity in every sense, we are to be pointed in that same direction. What is called for, then, is the maintaining of the tension of growth, rather than arrival at a stage of being holy where we no longer are capable of sin. So perfectionism as a state of sinlessness is not the goal of union, but is rather the direction of maturity needed to maintain the tension of growth in Christ within us.

In the same way, union is not just an ultimate 'second blessing' that will finally perfect the saints of God. It is not the ultimate 'experience' which is to be sought at all costs. This makes of the experience something to be worshipped, ignoring the God of all spiritual experiences. The writers of the spiritual guides knew what it was to worship at the shrine of religious experiences, so that each time one went to a religious meeting one was looking for a replica of the last great moment with God, or hoping that God would 'zap' him with an even greater experience than the last time. That makes of God an object, and of the experience, the end.

It is true that God allows us to experience tremendous joys and celebrations, but they are given that we might be drawn closer to Him and then learn to do without them. We are to come to that moment when we serve God whether we feel good or not; whether we have a religious high or must continue out of faithfulness amid darkness, dryness, and discouragements. Union may involve experiences of sensory elation, but they are only the outer garments of ourselves which must not be depended on as we experience in Christ a deep, abiding, interior joy and peace.

Neither is union a description of an event for a restricted few. As Paul has indicated, the windows of heaven have been thrown wide open and now all people everywhere can know the secrets of God: 'which is the secret he hid through all past ages from all mankind, but has now revealed to his people.

133

God's plan is to make known his secret to his people, this rich and glorious secret which he has for all peoples. And the secret is that Christ is in you, which means that you will share the glory of God. So we preach Christ to everyone. With all possible wisdom we warn and teach them in order to bring each one into God's presence as a mature individual in union with Christ' (Col. 1.26–28, GNB). Union, therefore, is not for the few initiates, but for all those who will open themselves up to God in loving attentiveness to His every word.

Jesus expressed the invitation to union in His farewell discourse as recorded in John's Gospel:

> I am the real vine, and my Father is the gardener. He breaks off every branch in me that does not bear fruit, and he prunes every branch that does bear fruit, so that it will be clean and bear more fruit. You have been made clean already by the teaching I have given you. Remain united to me, and I will remain united to you. A branch cannot bear fruit by itself; it can do so only if it remains in the vine. In the same way you cannot bear fruit unless you remain in me.
>
> I am the vine, and you are the branches. Whoever remains in me and I in him, will bear much fruit, for you can do nothing without me. Whoever does not remain in me is thrown out like a branch and dries up; such branches are gathered up and thrown into the fire, where they are burned (John 15.1–6, GNB).

Union is living attentively to God, living in God's Presence each moment as fully as we are capable and aware, as He reveals Himself to us in the mystery of each experience. Brother Lawrence, a seventeenth-century monk, was asked how he seemed to be able to live so close to God. He replied, 'We should establish ourselves in a sense of God's Presence by continually conversing with Him'.[1] He felt 'It was a shameful thing to quit His conversation to think of trifles and fooleries'.[2] He said that too many 'amused themselves with trivial devotions'[3] rather than learning to know God's Presence in each moment and in every activity as fully as when they were in the chapel at worship. He said that with him the 'set times of prayer were not different from other times . . . because his greatest business did not divert him from God.'[4] He further stated that too many felt they were obliged to pray only at the specified times set for prayer, but that

> his prayer was nothing else but a sense of the presence of God . . . and that when the appointed times of prayer were past, he found no difference, because he still continued with God, praising and blessing Him with all his might, so that he passed his life in continual joy.[5]

Finally, it was said of Brother Lawrence:

> In the greatest hurry of business in the kitchen he still preserved his recollection and heavenly-mindedness. He was never hasty nor loitering, but did each thing in its season, with an even, uninterrupted composure and tranquility of spirit. 'The time of business,' he said, 'does not with me differ from the time of prayer; and in the noise and clatter of my kitchen, while several persons are at the same time calling for different things, I possess God in as great tranquillity as if I were upon my knees [in chapel].'[6]

The nineteenth-century Russian Orthodox monk, Theophan, reflected this same attitude of attentiveness to God in all things. He advised others that,

> Into every duty a God-fearing heart must be put, a heart constantly permeated by the thought of God; and this will be the door through which the soul will enter into active life. All endeavour must be directed towards the ceaseless

thought of God, towards the constant awareness of His presence; 'Seek the Lord . . . Seek his face constantly (Psalm 105.4).'[7]

A thirteenth-century bishop of Thessalonia stated that this attentiveness to God was for lay persons as well as clergy:

For when we are engaged in manual labour and when we walk or sit down, when we eat or when we drink, we can always pray inwardly and practise prayer of the mind, true prayer, pleasing to God. Let us work with our body and pray with our soul. Let our outer man perform physical work, and let the inner man be consecrated wholly and completely to the service of God and never flag in the spiritual work of inner prayer.[8]

Union, therefore, is a standing before God all day long in a loving attentiveness, regardless of what activity we may be involved in. It is a listening in expectant awareness to know the depths of God who is revealing Himself from moment to moment. It is an entering into a loving dialogue with God in each circumstance of the day. It is being aware that, as God comes to us, it is pure gift and not something that we can cause to happen. It is a sensitivity that awaits God's comings and goings throughout the day, as it is constantly fixed on His loving gaze. It is saying with the psalmist, 'I walk in the presence of the Lord in the world of the living' (Ps. 116.9; compare 56.13, GNB).

Union is a co-operative dependence on God that leads out into our actions in the world. With this constant dependence on Him, we

live in an awareness of direct dependence on God—almost without realizing consciously, at every moment, how much we depend on Him; and receive from Him directly everything that comes to us as pure gift; and experience, taste in our hearts, the love of God in this gift, the delicacy and the personal attention of God to us in His merciful love.[9]

Union is not demanding that God come to us; it is a waiting in darkness and silence. It is a letting go of all that would keep us from knowing Him and being known by Him. It is an emptying of the false self. As Paul said, 'You have stripped off your old behaviour with your old self, and you have put on a new self which will progress toward true knowledge the more it is renewed in the image of its creator' (Col. 3.10, JB).

Union is not trying to get a particular experience or message that we want to hear out of God, but a waiting and listening in silence, a total *disponibilitá* to God. It is a living with the mystery of the ways of God in this world. It is being aware that the depths of God are higher than our thoughts, and the ways of God are a bewilderment to our rational categories.

Ours is the task of disposing and making ready the vessel. God gives as He will. We wait in abandonment, emptiness, and poverty of our own capabilities. We do not buy favours with our efforts. We don't seek union as if we had to make 'the first team'. We wait resting in His presence, seeking His face, knowing that as we are available, He comes to us in each and every circumstance of each moment of the day.

Living out of the depths in an active ministry and witness in the world is working and living in the world in that same degree of inwardness that we know during those moments of quiet each day and on retreat. As we work, we are to reflect that same degree of attentiveness and awareness of God as we do when God speaks to us in the moments of quiet.

We are not called to exploit the depths of God for bigger and better programmes but to realize an integrity of action and our quiet, contemplative moments so that our activity has the same contemplative depth as our inner life. Then, God will give us those things that He wishes for us to have, and we will be ready for them.

'Out of his infinite glory, may he give you the power through his Spirit for your hidden self to grow strong, so that Christ may live in your hearts through faith, and then, planted in love and built on love, you will with all the saints have strength to grasp the breadth and the length, the height and the depth; until, knowing the love of Christ, which is beyond all knowledge, you are filled with the utter fullness of God' (Eph. 3.16–19, JB).

Meditation Exercises

This week make plans for the meditation times that you will have the next several weeks, months, or a year. One way to do this would be to choose the meditative Scriptures you will work with either from the Gospels (Matthew, Mark, Luke, or John), the Psalms, the letters of Paul (especially Corinthians, Ephesians, Galatians, or Philippians) or the Pastoral Letters (James, Peter, or John). If you choose to work with the Gospels, you can either go straight through, or you can work with major events (stories or a selection of parables) in them. If you choose the Psalms, you may want to scan them first, selecting only eight or ten to work with. Choose only those which are meaningful to you, and then add others later.

You have already developed some skills in what to do in your daily quiet time, and these can be continued and added to later. Refer back to each chapter if you forget what to do, and refresh your memory with what might be helpful when you bog down. Begin now to search out some of the devotional classics and add them to your daily reading. Use the hymn book as a valuable resource in adding to your daily Scripture meditations.

Soon you will discover that you have developed your own

style for your daily quiet time. That is as it should be. What you have been doing daily has exposed you to some elements that will help you live that life deeply enough in a loving attentiveness to God's presence in your life.

How much time you spend in your daily quiet time will depend on you. You can gauge it by how much time is necessary for you to live at the depths of awareness of God in your life. You will find that it will vary depending on the work you are involved in, what's happening around you and to you, your capacity to be sensitive to God's presence, and the hunger there is within you. Allow the skills that you have begun developing these past few weeks to begin claiming you and become firmly rooted in you as God works out His creativity in you—as He unfolds to you a life lived out of the depths.

Notes

INTRODUCTION

1. For more information on formative spirituality, see the books by Adrian van Kaam, especially the volumes of *Formative Spirituality* (New York: Crossroads, 1983, 1984, 1986).

2. For additional information about keeping a spiritual journal see: Morton T. Kelsey, *Adventure Inward:* Christian Growth Through Personal Journal Writing (Minneapolis, Minn.: Augsburg, 1980) and George F. Simons, *Keeping Your Personal Journal* (New York: Paulist, 1978).

3. Spiritual direction, or being a spiritual friend, is an ancient form of guiding spiritual growth. It has received renewed attention in recent years as the following books reflect: Kenneth Leech, *Soul Friend*: The Practice of Christian Spirituality (London: Sheldon Press, 1977); Tilden Edwards, *Spiritual Friend*: Reclaiming the Gift of Spiritual Direction (New York: Paulist, 1980); Alan Jones, *Exploring Spiritual Direction* (New York: Seabury, 1982); Alan Jones, *Soul Making* (San Francisco: Harper and Row, 1985).

CHAPTER I

1. Elizabeth O'Connor, *Our Many Selves* (New York: Harper and Row, 1971), p. 59.

2. John Sanford, *The Kingdom Within* (New York: J.B. Lippincott Co., 1970), p. 21. Reprinted by permission of J.B. Lippincott Company.

3. Thomas Merton, *New Seeds of Contemplation* (New York: New Directions, 1961), p. 295. This and subsequent quotations are copyright © 1961 by The Abbey of Gethsemani, Inc. Reprinted by permission of New Directions Publishing Corporation. Two other writers have described self-identity as a transcendent issue: Louis Dupre, *Transcendent Selfhood*: The Rediscovery of the Inner Life (New York: Seabury, 1976); and Adrian van Kaam,

The Transcendent Self (Denville, N.J.: Dimension Books, 1979).

4. Merton, p. 33.

5. Ibid., pp. 33–34.

6. Frank Stagg, 'Matthew', *Broadman Bible Commentary* (Nashville: Broadman Press, 1969), 8.177.

7. Merton, p. 33.

8. As quoted in Thomas Kelly, *A Testament of Devotion* (New York: Harper and Row, 1941), p. 52.

9. Merton, p. 34.

10. Timothy Ware, ed., *The Art of Prayer* (London: Faber and Faber, 1966), p. 46.

11. Merton, p. 51.

12. Working with the Scriptures meditatively, or reflective reading, has been well described by Susan A. Muto: *Approaching the Sacred:* An Introduction to Spiritual Reading (Denville, N.J: Dimension Books, 1973) and *Steps Along the Way*: The Path of Spiritual Reading (Denville, N.J.: Dimension Books, 1975). See also M. Robert Mulholland, Jr., *Shaped By the Word:* The Power of Scripture in Spiritual Formation (Nashville: The Upper Room, 1985).

13. I do not claim originality for this meditation process. I first heard of it several years ago at the Church of the Saviour in Washington, D.C., but have been unable to locate its parentage. It seems to grow out of the Ignatian process.

CHAPTER 2

1. Theological foundations for spirituality are necessary. Recent writers have given us theological frameworks within which to examine spirtuality: Kenneth Leech, *True God*: An Exploration in Spirituality (London: Sheldon Press, 1985); Francis Baur, *Life in Abundance*: A Contemporary Spirituality (New York: Paulist Press, 1983); and Frank C. Senn., ed., *Protestant Spiritual Traditions* (New York: Paulist, 1986).

2. Douglas V. Steere, *On Beginning From Within/On Listening to Another* (New York: Harper and Row, 1964), pp. 198–199.

3. Martin Buber, *I and Thou*, trans., Walter Kaufmann (Edinburgh: T. & T. Clark, 1971), pp. 32 ff, 39 ff.

4. Malcolm Muggeridge, *Something Beautiful for God* (London: Fontana, 1972).

5. This foundational disposition to Christian growth is most beautifully described by Adrian van Kaam in *Spirituality and the Gentle Life* (Denville, N.J.: Dimension Books, 1974).

CHAPTER 3

1. Thomas Merton, *New Seeds of Contemplation* (New York: New Directions, 1961). p. 15.

2. Ibid.

3. Ibid., pp. 192–193.

4. Thomas à Kempis, *The Imitation of Christ*, Betty I. Knott, trans., (London: Collins, 1963), p. 135.

5. Thomas Merton, *Thoughts in Solitude* (London: Burns Oates, 1975), p. 81.

6. Quoted in Edward J. Farrell, *Disciples and Other Strangers* (Denville, New Jersey: Dimension Books, 1974), pp. 147–148. This quotation is copyright © 1974 by Dimension Books. Reprinted by permission of Edward J. Farrell.

CHAPTER 4

1. Thomas Merton, *Contemplative Prayer* (London: Darton, Longman and Todd, 1975), p. 41. This and subsequent quotations are copyright © 1975 by Darton, Longman and Todd Ltd. and are used by permission of the publishers

CHAPTER 5

1. Our goal is a more transcendent, reflective way of living. For a good description of this, see Claire Brissette, *Reflective Living: A Spiritual Approach to Everyday Life* (Whitinsville, Mass.: Affirmation Books, 1983).

CHAPTER 6

1. Søren Kierkegaard, *Purity of Heart*, Douglas V. Steere, trans. (New York: Harper and Row, 1948).

2. E. Glenn Hinson, *A Serious Call To A Contemplative Lifestyle* (Philadelphia: Westminster Press, 1974), pp. 63, 78.

3. William Stringfellow, *An Ethic for Christians and Other Aliens In A Strange Land* (Waco: Word Books, 1973), p. 138.

4. Thomas Merton, *New Seeds of Contemplation* (New York: New Directions, 1961), p. 203.

5. Ibid.

6. Arthur W. Combs, Anne C. Richards, Fred Richards, *Perceptual Psychology* (New York: Harper and Row, 1976), p. 106 ff.

7. Henri Nouwen *Pray to Live* (Notre Dame, Ind.: Fides, 1972), p. 51.

CHAPTER 7

1. Spiritual disciplines have received much attention since the publication by Quaker Richard J. Foster, *Celebration of Discipline*. Others who have also stated the disciplines for spiritual growth are: James C. Fenhagen, *More Than Wanderers:* Christian Disciplines for Christian Ministry (New York: Seabury Press, 1978); Ronald V. Well, *Spiritual Disciplines for Everyday Living* (Schenectady, NY: Character Research Press, 1982); and Susan A. Muto, *Pathways of Spiritual Living* (Garden City, N.Y.: Doubleday, 1984).

2. Elizabeth O'Connor first described these disciplines in *Call to Commitment* (New York: Harper and Row, 1963), p. 34.

3. George A. Maloney, *A Return to Fasting* (Pecos, New Mexico: Dove, 1974), p. 15.

4. Ibid.

5. Thomas Merton, *Contemplative Prayer* (London: Darton, Longman and Todd), p. 73.

CHAPTER 9

1. This quotation from 'The Continuing Effect of the American Revolution' by Arnold J. Toynbee, given on the occasion of the Celebration of The Prelude to Independence, June 10, 1961 at Williamsburg, Virginia, is copyright © 1962 by H.W. Wilson and Company in *Representative American Speeches* and used by permission.

2. Ibid.

CHAPTER 10

1. Thomas Kelly, *A Testament of Devotion* (New York: Harper and Row, 1941), p. 109.

2. Ibid.

3. Ira Progoff, *Jung's Psychology and Its Social Meaning* (New York: Doubleday/Anchor, 1953–73), p. 161.

4. Gordon Cosby, *Handbook For Mission Groups* (Waco: Word Books, 1975), p. 16.

5. Malcolm Muggeridge, *Something Beautiful for God* (London: Fontana, 1972), pp. 19, 84.

6. Pierre Teilhard de Chardin, *Building the Earth* (New York: Avon Books, 1969), p. 35.

7. Dallas Lee, *The Cotton Patch Evidence* (New York: Harper and Row, 1971).

8. Rollo May, *The Courage to Create* (New York: W.W. Norton and Co., 1975).

CHAPTER 11

1. Johannes B. Metz, *Poverty of Spirit* (New York: Newman Press, 1968), p. 16.

2. John Haughey, *The Conspiracy of God* (New York: Doubleday, 1973), p. 61

CHAPTER 12

1. Brother Lawrence, *The Practice of the Presence of God* (Old Tappan, N.J.: Fleming H. Revell Co., 1958).

2. Ibid.

3. Ibid.

4. Ibid.

5. Ibid.

6. Ibid.

7. E. Kadoubousky and E.M. Palmer, trans., *The Art of Prayer* (London: Faber and Faber, 1966), pp. 85–86.

8. Ibid., p. 87.

9. Thomas Merton, *Contemplation In A World of Action* (New York: Doubleday Image, 1973), p. 386.

Unless otherwise indicated, Bible quotations are the author's translation.